MW00617546

# Home Computers Can Make You Rich

JOE WEISBECKER

## HAYDEN BOOK COMPANY, INC.
Rochelle Park, New Jersey

For Jean
my partner in everything

*Library of Congress Cataloging in Publication Data*

Weisbecker, Joe.
    Home computers can make you rich.

    Includes index.
    1. Small business—Handbooks, manuals, etc.
2. Self-employed—Handbooks, manuals, etc.
3. Microcomputers—Handbooks, manuals, etc.
I. Title
HF5356.W28          658'.04'1          79-25984
ISBN  0-8104-5177-8

*Copyright © 1980 by Joseph Weisbecker.* All rights reserved. No part of this book may be reprinted, or reproduced, or utilized in any form or by any electronic, mechanical, or other means, now known or hereafter invented, including photocopying and recording, or in any information storage and retrieval system, without permission in writing from the Publisher.

*Printed in the United States of America*

            4  5  6  7  8  9   PRINTING

    81 82 83 84 85 86 87 88   YEAR

# Preface

Low-cost microcomputers are creating hundreds of new ways for you to make money in your spare time. This book describes many of these new opportunities and shows you how to take advantage of them. You'll find ideas you can use whether you're a home computer beginner or a microcomputer expert. You can even make extra money without owning a computer. Isn't it time for you to learn more about a fascinating new hobby that might also make you rich?

You'll be introduced to the microcomputer industry and some types of people involved in it. You'll find out how to learn more about this new industry. Some basic principles of making money will be reviewed. You'll learn about freelance writing, programming, consulting, and inventing. Ideas for articles, books, programs, games, gadgets, arts, crafts, tools, services, attachments, computer-made products, investing, and speculating will be discussed. There is something here for every home computer owner and for nonowners who are interested in new spare-time income opportunities. Here's your chance to get in on the ground floor of a major new industry and grab a piece of the action. Opportunities like this come along only once in a lifetime.

This book assumes some familiarity with computers. Chapter 3 lists some references that might be helpful if you are a beginner. I have a tendency to forget that there are people who don't know about home computers yet. I have made some attempt to avoid computer jargon, but it still creeps in occasionally.

The advice, philosophy, and ideas offered in this book are based on years of personal trial-and-error experience as opposed to secondhand theory. As the bottom line of a stockbroker's tip sheet always says, "Past performance can't always guarantee future success." It is up to you to evaluate, select, and modify these ideas so that they will work for you.

# Contents

# 1

# The Microcomputer Industry

## A New Industry Is Born

Large computers costing hundreds of thousands of dollars have been around since the 1930s. Only big companies and government agencies could afford them then. Minicomputers costing $50,000 or less became available in the 1960s. Large numbers of medium-size companies could afford minicomputers. In the 1970s microcomputers costing several hundred to several thousand dollars started to appear. At these prices most small businesses and even individual homes could afford a computer. Low-cost, mass-produced microcomputers represent a major new industry. This rapidly growing industry provides many opportunities for new job, business, product, and spare-time income.

Just as the development of the internal combustion engine made the automobile possible, the development of large-scale integrated circuits made the low-cost microcomputer possible. This large-scale integration (LSI) technology permits very complex electronic circuits containing thousands of transistors to be fabricated cheaply in the form of a tiny silicon chip smaller than your fingernail. In turn, these chips permit the size and cost of computers to be dramatically reduced. A single chip costing only a few dollars can provide most of the control circuitry required for a computer. Other chips can provide the necessary memory circuits. Combining a few such chips with appropriate input and output devices results in a complete microcomputer. Input-output devices can include keyboards, displays, printers, and disc or magnetic tape units for data storage.

The uses of a specific computer are limited by its input-output capabilities. A computer without a printer obviously cannot be used to type letters or paychecks. A computer without a disc storage device cannot be used effectively for many data-processing applications. Mechanical input-output devices can add significantly to the cost of a microcomputer.

Any computer can be programmed to perform a wide range of operations within the limitations imposed by its input-output capabilities.

The uses of a specific computer are therefore limited by available programs as well as by the computer's physical capabilities. Growth of the microcomputer industry will depend on the continuing development of new techniques for low-cost input-output and data storage coupled with imaginative programming. These two areas represent major profit opportunities for companies and individuals.

When the automobile industry is mentioned, one immediately thinks of Ford, General Motors, and Chrysler. In the microcomputer industry most of the attention is focused on the companies that make small computers. Because it's unlikely that your spare-time road to riches will involve manufacturing computers, you'll need to take a broader view of the microcomputer industry.

The major car makers are only part of the entire automotive industry. The industry also includes thousands of other companies and individuals who prosper by filling needs not satisfied by the companies that produce cars. Among them are local car dealers, individual salesmen, used car lots, independent shopping guides, and consultants to fill the needs of car buyers. Potential car users can rent a car or a driver. Car customizing, painting, racing, and repairing provide full or part-time income for many people. Supplying parts, fuel, accessories, and disposal are other sources of income. Freelance writers and inventors derive income from the car industry. We've only scratched the surface, but you probably get the idea. To find spare-time money-making opportunities in the microcomputer industry you must look for needs not satisfied by the companies that make the microcomputers. This book will help you to identify these needs and show you how to satisfy them for fun and profit in your spare time.

Before proceeding with the mundane business of making money, you should become familiar with the four basic types of microcomputers.

## The Four Types of Microcomputers

The microcomputer industry is comprised of two major segments. One segment involves computers for small businesses, and the other relates to small computers for home use. These two segments overlap to some extent. There is plenty of action in both areas for anyone interested in spare-time income opportunities. This book emphasizes the home computer segment with a few carefully selected excursions into the business segment.

Microcomputers can also be classified as *general purpose* or *special purpose* computers. This gives us four basic types of microcomputers:

Type 1—General purpose for business or industrial use.

Type 2—Special purpose for business or industrial use.

Type 3—General purpose for home or hobby use.

Type 4—Special purpose for home or hobby use.

Let's look at the major differences among these four types of microcomputers. A general purpose computer can be programmed by its owner, which means that the owner of a general purpose computer can easily modify its operation to suit his changing needs. It also means that a manufacturer can mass produce one low-cost general purpose computer that will suit a variety of owner needs. Different programs tailor it to different owners. General purpose computers are generally designed with expansibility in mind. That is, you can easily add extra data storage capability or new input-output devices when they are needed.

Special purpose computers are designed for a limited set of operations. Their programs are built in by the manufacturer and are not easily modified by the owner. They usually have limited memory and specialized input-output capabilities that can't be easily expanded by the owner. There must be a large number of customers with the same application needs to justify producing a special purpose computer to satisfy these needs. Modern electronic calculators, video games, traffic light controllers, and cash registers are typical examples of special purpose microcomputers. General purpose computers tend to be more expensive than special purpose computers. The ability to change programs and expand input-output or storage capability adds to the cost of general purpose computers.

Business computers are usually more expensive than home computers for several reasons. First, the cost of a business computer is usually justified on the basis of tangible savings to the owner. For example, suppose the annual salary of a file clerk is $7,000 and the salary of a clerk who can operate a computer is $9,000. Over a two-year period two file clerks cost the business $28,000. If a computer operator and a microcomputer could replace the two file clerks, then it would cost the business $18,000 plus the price of the microcomputer over the same two-year period. The business would break even, or save money, if the microcomputer cost $10,000 or less. It is hard to set a similar tangible value on a home computer used for recreational, educational, or hobby purposes. As a result the market for home computers is apt to be much more price sensitive than the market for computers for small businesses.

Another reason for the price difference between business and home computers is the quality of construction or reliability required. Business computers usually receive heavier use, and failures can be catastrophic to the business. Home use generally involves lighter use; failures are merely inconvenient. Higher quality and reliability requirements add to the cost of microcomputers designed primarily for business use.

A third cost factor involves the uses for home and business computers. Business use generally requires larger data storage capability, faster access to stored data, and printed output. Many home applications require only output on a TV screen and less demanding storage capability. Again, the added performance requirements add to the cost of the business microcomputer.

The microcomputer industry is based on the four types of computers listed earlier. The general purpose, business-oriented microcomputer is usually the most expensive type, with current prices being in the $2,000 to $10,000 range. The special purpose microcomputer aimed at home use tends to be the least expensive type, with prices in the $10 to $500 range. Calculators and handheld electronic games fall in the lower end of this price range. At the top end are the elaborate video games and electronic home pinball machines. If you are going to use a microcomputer in your spare-time money-making activities, it will probably be a general purpose type.

Currently, a typical, minimum-cost, general purpose home computer costs $600 to $1,000. It has a keyboard with which to enter data and programs. Internal memory capacity is in the range of 4,000 to 16,000 bytes, or characters. Output is in the form of words, numbers, and pictures displayed on a TV screen. An audio cassette recorder lets you store data and programs for later use. The computer is probably programmed in a language called BASIC. In the future the price of a microcomputer system of this type might drop to the $200 to $600 range.

The minimum cost for a typical, general purpose, business-oriented microcomputer system is currently about $2,500. It has a keyboard for data entry and an internal memory capacity of 16,000 to 32,000 bytes, or characters. Both printed and TV screen outputs are provided. External data or program storage is provided by a magnetic disc device. Again, this system is programmed in BASIC. The future price for this type of system might drop to $1,500.

Several currently available microcomputers are described in Chapter 4. Just keep in mind that the microcomputer industry is based on the four types listed earlier on page 4. You should also remember that these four types of microcomputers reflect the different needs of various market segments.

## Hardware Hackers and Programmers

The microcomputer industry includes products and people. To make money you should know something about both. Hardware hackers and programmers are two types of people you should become familiar with. They are potential customers, and you will eventually become one of them if you are serious about making money in the microcomputer industry.

Hardware hackers like to play with transistor circuits, build electronic gadgets, and learn how things work. They enjoy designing, modifying, or repairing computers. Hardware hackers build kits and find new uses for existing devices and parts. Electronic experimenters, engineers, technicians, and repairmen are hardware hackers. Most pioneers in home computers are hardware hackers. They read technical magazines and books. Companies such as Heath and Radio Shack cater to their needs.

Hardware hackers need books and articles that tell them how to build new electronic gadgets, how to fix or modify their computer, and how to control physical devices with a computer. They buy electronic construction kits, tools, test instruments, and parts. Articles, books, and information on inventing or how things work appeal to them. The number of hardware hackers is limited by the relatively high level of knowledge and skill required. Filling their specialized needs can be a financially rewarding spare-time activity with relatively little competition. You'll have to become a hardware hacker yourself to succeed in this area.

Programmers get their satisfaction from designing computer programs. In many cases they don't even use the programs they develop. The fun and challenge involve proving that they can make a computer do what they want it to. If you crossed a cowardly lion trainer with a crossword puzzle solver, you would probably get a programmer. The art of programming can provide a fascinating hobby or career. Programming provides the same mental challenge as playing chess. Many programmers are also mathematicians. Before the availability of low-cost home computers, most programmers were limited to playing with large computers owned by their school or employer. These professional programmers have been among the first people to buy inexpensive home computers. Because they have been "spoiled" by experience with large computers, they are the leaders in complaining about the limitations imposed on them by low-cost home computers. Programmers also like to argue about the merits of various programming languages. They spend large amounts of time designing operating systems, editing systems, and other programming tools just in case they want to write a useful application program some day. The ranks of programmers are growing more rapidly than hardware hackers because of the relative ease with which a beginner can learn programming.

Programmers need articles, books, and information on programming techniques, new computer languages, and new types of programs. They buy attachments to increase the capabilities of their computer and utility programs to make programming and debugging easier. Along with hardware hackers, they provide a market for computer-related gadgets, posters, and T-shirts. As new, lower-cost, easier-to-program computers become available, the number of programmers of home computers will grow rapidly. Learning to program will be necessary if you want to maximize your spare-time income opportunities.

Hardware hackers and programmers seem to have one thing in common—an avid curiosity about the others' specialty. Hardware hackers are anxious to learn about programming techniques, and programmers usually want to learn more about hardware. This provides you with an opportunity to write tutorial hardware articles aimed at programmers and software articles aimed at hardware hackers. You should keep in mind that your market will be comprised of people with interests and abilities in both areas. It is also helpful to divide hardware hackers and programmers into three skill levels—beginner, intermediate, and advanced. Beginning and intermediate programmers will comprise the largest group, whereas advanced hardware hackers will form the smallest group of potential customers for your products or services.

Identifying your market by specific interest and skill level will help you in designing and selling appropriate products or services. If you're aiming at advanced hardware hackers or programmers, you should stress newness, novelty, multiple options, or ability to customize for your product. If you're aiming at beginners, stress ease of use and low cost. There are magazines slanted toward beginning hardware hackers and others aimed at intermediate programmers. Knowing which group your customers belong in will tell you where to advertise your product or service.

Providing products and services that will appeal to hardware hackers and programmers is a proven, spare-time, money-making activity. Some larger markets for you to consider are discussed next.

### Users and Nonowners

Many microcomputer owners or potential owners aren't interested in how computers work or how to program them. They are interested only in what the microcomputer will do for them. If they buy a general purpose computer, they want someone else to program it for them. These people represent a major market for special purpose computers and ready-to-use, general purpose computer programs. Most of the business market for microcomputers falls into the category of users. Lawyers, real estate agencies, doctors, or small stores don't buy microcomputers to play with or program. They buy them to save time or money in their businesses. Computer stores and software publishers satisfy this desire by providing microcomputer programs for standard bookkeeping and data-processing functions common to most businesses. Companies satisfy this need by providing special purpose microcomputers in the form of medical instruments and cash registers.

Although the business segment of the microcomputer market offers a variety of money-making opportunities, it is difficult for a beginner to take advantage of them. Business customers want immediate attention and may be reluctant to depend on a part-time hobbyist. Dealing with hard-nosed business clients isn't much fun and could make excessive demands on your time. Most computer stores, companies, and professional consultants are currently aiming their efforts at the small business market, and you will be faced with stiff competition. After due consideration, you will probably conclude that the best initial opportunities for spare-time income exist in the home computer segment of the market. After all, you'll have first-hand experience as a home computer owner yourself. Later on you may develop the skills required to compete in the small business area.

Large numbers of people will purchase general purpose micro-computers for home use. Some will be hardware hackers or programmers. Many more will be users who are interested only in what the computer will do for them. They want it for education, entertainment, saving time, making money, improving the quality of life, or impressing friends. They immediately discover that they need programs to satisfy these desires. Some will become programmers. Most will want to obtain a continuing supply of new programs for their computer without becoming programmers themselves. Standard languages such as BASIC don't become popular just because they make programming easier. They are popular because computer users can obtain programs for their computers without doing any programming at all. They can obtain these programs in the form of tape cassettes, books, or magazine articles. You can make money by designing new programs in your spare time. Of course, these programs should be those that a lot of people will want to use on their computers. Chapter 6 discusses writing and selling programs in more detail.

Potential microcomputer owners represent another large market segment. These people need to learn more about microcomputers and why they should own one. Writing articles that tell them about microcomputers can be a profitable spare-time activity. Giving lectures and demonstrations or teaching a microcomputer course at an evening school can put extra dollars in your pocket. People who are interested in buying a home computer but who can't justify the cost can often afford computer-related games, gadgets, and T-shirts. Many people won't realize that they want a computer until you develop the type of program that appeals to them. Computer companies are always looking for programs that will help them sell computers. Your new computer application might even be patentable in the form of a special purpose microcomputer. Somebody has to invent next year's hot new electronic game or toy—why not you?

With your own computer you can provide a variety of products and services for people who are not even interested in microcomputers. You might print their Christmas card labels, calculate their horoscopes, or provide entertainment at their parties. You can even use your computer to tutor their children. People who don't own general purpose microcomputers will outnumber those who do for a long time. Chapters 7 and 8 give you more ideas for profitable products and services aimed at nonowners.

## Trend Watching for Fun and Profit

Keeping track of new developments and trends is part of any hobby or successful business. The microcomputer industry is evolving so rapidly that watching it closely is especially important if you want to find new spare-time money-making opportunities. To be successful you will have to learn to spot trends, recognize potential dead ends, and predict the popularity of new products.

There are all sorts of trends to watch. You should be aware of trends toward specific languages, microcomputers, and types of applications. Cost trends are particularly important. Demographic trends can tell you which age and income segments of the market are growing. Popular fads or trends such as biorhythm, astrology, or home security can give you ideas for articles, books, programs, or attachments that will be popular. Trends toward new input-output devices can open up new opportunities for you. Economic trends influence what people will buy. High rates of inflation should provide a large market for microcomputer programs to help people make or save money. A national trend toward gambling provides a market for computerized betting or handicapping systems.

Early recognition of the trend toward BASIC as a popular microcomputer programming language would have provided the opportunity to write tutorial books and articles. There are now so many beginner BASIC books that your chances of interesting a publisher in another one are pretty small. Other languages may gain in popularity as programmers become bored with BASIC and new microcomputers appear. Early recognition of a new language trend will again open up the market for tutorial material.

The availability of new microcomputers will provide you with another set of opportunities, providing you can predict winners. Evaluate new microcomputers in terms of company, price, and function in order to predict winners. Is the company financially sound? Does it have adequate marketing, distribution, and customer-servicing capability? Can it manufacture in volume? Does the new computer have a significantly lower cost than other popular products in its class? Does it use the latest technology so that it won't become obsolete too soon? Does it provide obviously desirable new features at a low price? If the answer to these questions is yes, then you should consider buying the new microcomputer as well as stock in the company. New user groups, newsletters, programs, articles, and books will also be in demand.

Microcomputer cost is a critical factor to watch. The home computer market is extremely price sensitive. Each time a less expensive product appears, the number of microcomputer owners increases dramatically. Even more important, the number of viable applications increases. There are many potential computer applications that can't be justified at the current prices of general purpose microcomputers. If a large number of potential customers is involved, a less expensive special purpose computer might be justified, as was the case with calculators and video games. There are, however, many specialized computer applications that involve markets too small to justify the design of a special purpose microcomputer. Cheaper, general purpose microcomputers will provide you with new opportunities in these small, specialized markets.

For example, renting a computer for parties is probably a relatively small business opportunity. If your computer costs you $2,000, you cannot set your rental fee low enough to attract customers and still show a profit. If you could obtain a suitable computer for $200, this application might become an excellent spare-time income opportunity. Keep your eye on microcomputer price trends to spot new possibilities for applications.

In the area of small markets you have a major advantage over large companies. They can't afford to develop products or services for small, specialized, or local markets, but you can. Your overhead is low, and you don't have to make as much money to stay in business. Always be on the lookout for small markets that can provide you with a big spare-time income. Becoming an expert in several small specialized areas can give you a competitive edge.

Trends can help you in other ways. You should examine the markets that are left behind by a popular new trend. As new microcomputers appear, there is a rush to buy them, write about them, and develop uses or programs for them. Left behind temporarily are owners of older, less popular microcomputers. Because this group tends to shrink with time, it is often ignored. After all, who's interested in providing products and services for a shrinking market? The answer may be you. Owners of older microcomputers can still use new programs or attachments, and your competition in providing them will be minimal. Don't ignore this spare-time profit opportunity. At the same time be ready to move on to another area before your market disappears entirely.

In the next chapter we discuss some of the basic principles involved in making money. Armed with these principles and an understanding of the microcomputer industry, you'll be ready to start down the road toward financial freedom.

# 2

## What You Need to Know about Making Money

### Four Basic Ways to Make Money

To make money you can sell products, sell services, create new products, or gamble. The microcomputer industry provides opportunities for you to pick up extra money in any of these four ways. All the ideas in this book are based on these four approaches to making money. Let's take a brief look at each approach.

Selling products related to microcomputers can be a profitable spare-time activity. You can sell existing products or new ones that you create. Products might consist of programs, computer jewelery, arts and crafts, information booklets, or electronic kits. An imaginative choice of products and novel marketing techniques can give you an advantage over your competition. You can sell products through direct personal contact, computer stores, or advertising in magazines or newsletters. Selling products involves developing product sources, maintaining an inventory, advertising, and filling orders. Direct involvement in selling products or filling orders will require a certain amount of your time per sale. Make sure your prices include the value of your time.

Selling services related to microcomputers can also be a profitable spare-time activity for you. Local services such as kit building, custom programming, microcomputer repair, or part-time teaching involve selling your time. You will, of course, have to develop a saleable skill. The amount of money you can make will be determined by your ability and the amount of time you can spend. Another type of service involves renting your microcomputer to people for recreational or educational purposes. This approach doesn't use up as much of your time, but it does require an initial investment in hardware.

Creating new products is an ideal way to earn extra money. Writing books, developing new programs, and inventing new computer-related games or gadgets are examples. You can devote as much or as little time to

11

to this activity as you desire. The amount of money you can make is determined by the popularity of your new product and not by the amount of time you spend creating it. You can sell your new product yourself or let someone else make and sell it. The latter course of action is often best for you. For example, you might develop a new microcomputer program and find a publisher to produce and sell it on a royalty basis. Your time is then free to create more new products while your first creation continues to earn money for you. The publisher of your program risks his time and money on your behalf. Using this type of leverage can multiply your money-making ability.

Gambling is the forth basic approach to making money. This involves letting your money work for you. Of course, you have to have some extra money to start with. Bankers and stockbrokers like to refer to this approach as investment. If you can risk some money, have nerves of steel, a touch of ESP, and are willing to learn the rules, you might consider part-time gambling. Microcomputers and gambling are a natural combination. The rapidly growing microcomputer industry provides opportunities for you to invest in new small businesses or to trade the stock of larger companies. Your own microcomputer might help you become a successful option trader or pork belly speculator. The amount of money you can make is limited only by your skill and luck. On the other hand, the amount of money you can lose is limited only by your credit rating.

### Two Money-Making Principles

If you are going to sell products, sell services, or create new ones, there are two basic principles you should know about:

1. Find a need and fill it at a reasonable cost.
2. Never overestimate the intelligence of your customers.

Products are successful because they satisfy the needs of the people who buy them. The more people with needs satisfied by your product, the larger your market. Your customer must, of course, realize that he has a need for your product or service. For example, you might decide there is a real need for a new programming language and proceed to develop one. You are subsequently amazed when you can't sell it. The reason is simple: Your potential customers don't realize that they need your new language. The major job of salesmen and advertising is to convince customers that they need or want a specific product or service.

Before trying to sell an existing product, list all the possible needs or desires it might fill. Then look for specific types of customers who might be convinced that they have these needs. This approach will help you to find new markets for existing products. Selling existing audio cassette storage racks and video games in computer stores illustrates this approach. Advertising existing microcomputers with appropriate programs in gambling publications is another example.

Before creating a new product or service, decide who your customers will be. Define their needs and design your product or service to satisfy them. For example, before writing an article decide on which magazine you want to sell it to. Define the specific needs and interests of its readers. Design your article to appeal to the majority of these readers, and you'll have little trouble selling it.

Advertising for your product or service should always be aimed at filling needs. Professionals always slant their copy toward what a product or service will do for the potential customer. They stress saving money, making life easier, or becoming more popular instead of merely listing product specifications. They tell customers how the product will satisfy their needs or desires instead of just telling them what it is and how much it costs. If you are selling a blackjack program, include a description of a popular betting system. Tell your potential customers how your program will help them learn this system without risking any money. Tell them how this system can improve their chances to win when they visit Las Vegas or Atlantic City. Whatever you are trying to sell, be sure to tell people what it will do for them. "Sell the sizzle and not the steak" is an old sales motto that also applies to new microcomputer-related products.

It should be obvious that you must satisfy needs or desires at a reasonable price in order to make money. Every need has a price associated with it. This price is determined by what a customer is willing to pay to have a need or desire satisfied. The price you can charge has very little to do with what it costs you to provide a product or service. Your product price must always be based on its perceived value to a customer and the price of competitive products. Establish the optimum price for your product or service first. Then work backward to calculate the cost of providing it. Don't forget to include the value of your time. If your costs are significantly lower than the price you can charge, you should proceed. If not, you have three options. You can drop the idea, figure out how to reduce your costs, or come up with a way to raise the price. You can raise the price by increasing the perceived value to the customer.

Let's look at some specific examples. A magazine publisher might perceive the value of an article at $50 per page. If you want to make $10 an hour, you must limit yourself to writing articles that take less than five hours per page to prepare. You must drop ideas that take you more than five hours per page to write, or else you must settle for a lower hourly rate of pay. Suppose you want to sell a blackjack program by means of small ads in computer magazines. If similar programs are selling for $10, then you will have to sell yours for $10 or less no matter what your costs are. Suppose, however, that you include a description of various blackjack systems with your program as mentioned previously. Instead of a blackjack program, your product becomes a computer-aided course in winning at blackjack. The perceived value of this course might be considerably higher than $10. This permits you to charge a higher price than your competition, which is offering only a blackjack program.

Always remember to base your prices on perceived value to customers. Look for products or services whose perceived value is high and on which your costs are low. How you package or advertise your product can enhance its perceived value. Think of the cosmetic industry where a few cents worth of chemicals can be sold for $5 or $10 with the right packaging and advertising.

The second principle of making money states that you should never overestimate the intelligence of your customers. This principle applies to your product or service as well as to how you try to sell it. Most people avoid products that appear complex or difficult to understand and use. Companies that want to sell consumer products in large volume know that ease of use is a primary design goal. That's why color TV sets have automatic tuning and cameras have automatic focusing. Look at popular TV shows, magazines, and books to see this principle in action. Whether you're writing an article or designing a computer program, keep it easy to understand and use if you want to sell it.

You may create the best gadget, article, or program in the world; but if you overestimate the intelligence of your potential customers, they won't buy it. How many people would be anxious to buy a package containing small globular masses of acetylsalicylic acid? Don't you think more people would want to buy a box of pills that will cure headaches, relieve pain, and reduce fever? Always explain clearly to your customers in words they can understand exactly what your product or service will do for them. Don't assume that they already know. Avoid highly technical explanations and jargon. Plain English won't insult anyone, and you'll avoid limiting your market to a few experts. Most people have a fear of appearing stupid. They would rather simply avoid products they don't understand rather than admit they don't understand.

## Pitfalls and Problems

Spare-time money making should be treated like any other business activity. To show a profit you have to do the right things and avoid doing the wrong things. This section will help you to avoid some of the pitfalls along the road to achieving a spare-time fortune in the microcomputer industry. The first pitfall to avoid involves spending too much money unwisely. Initially, you should spend money only on educational items such as books and magazines. Chapter 3 gives you an idea of what is available. Before buying hardware, you should plan exactly what you will use it for. This planning should include the amount of money you expect to make with a specific piece of hardware. In other words, don't just run out and buy several different microcomputers hoping you'll figure out what to do with them later. It's to your advantage to delay purchase until you've decided exactly how you will use your microcomputer. Chapter 4 discusses some of the currently available microcomputers.

Ideally, you should expand your money-making activities out of profits. You could buy your first computer with money you've earned by selling articles, books, or ideas. Buying new hardware only out of current profits automatically limits your expenses to reasonable levels. You certainly don't want to end up owning a lot of expensive equipment that doesn't pay for itself. This attitude differentiates a serious part-time business from a typical hobby. Under no circumstances should you borrow money to get started in a spare-time venture. There are enough ways to bootstrap yourself up. Limited borrowing for expansion of a proven money-making venture is sometimes okay.

Forgetting to define your specific market and its needs can guarantee failure. Your degree of success will be directly related to the amount of time you devote to understanding your potential customers. The pitfalls for a beginner in the business segment of the microcomputer market have already been discussed.

Acting like an amateur can drastically reduce your chances for success. Publishers tend automatically to ignore manuscripts and letters written in pencil. Poor English and misspelled words don't impress book and magazine editors. Pencil-written correspondence on lined paper or the back of an envelope doesn't impress customers. Consultants who solicit business with letters of this type don't find much work. Programs with sloppy or incomplete user instructions don't generate repeat business. Program publishers might be more interested in buying programs from you if your documentation has a professional appearance. Companies usually avoid dealing with amateur inventors. Custom stationary and a carbon ribbon for your typewriter can help create a professional appearance. The wording of your letters should be designed to reinforce this appearance. Make sure that material you are trying to sell to individual customers or companies appears to be professionally prepared. Always act like a professional who knows what he is doing, and you'll be treated like one.

Avoid situations that involve excessive time and money risks. For example, publishing and selling your own book would probably involve excessive risks. It is generally better to let an existing publisher take these risks for you. He can spread his risk over a large number of books, not all of which must be successful. Because of your limited capital and time, you can't spread your risk. Finding someone else to sell a program you develop will give you free time to develop more new programs. If you have only a limited amount of spare time, you must allocate it wisely for maximum income.

Following the crowd can sometimes get you in trouble. Just because everyone is selling a Startrek program doesn't mean that you should develop one to sell. Jumping in on the tail end of a trend with another "me too" product is a sure way to fail. In the early days of microcomputers, a large number of small companies adopted a standard interface called the S–100 bus. Since then a number of larger companies have introduced computers that don't use this previous interface standard. Some of the smaller companies using it will probably disappear. If you are considering the development of new microcomputer attachments, you will have to evaluate carefully the advisability of using what may become an obsolete S-100 bus standard. Carefully evaluate the nature of any crowd you plan to follow. Make sure they aren't lemmings.

By all means avoid the "microcomputers can do everything" disease. It's highly contagious. New microcomputer owners often catch this disease. You'll find them in the back rooms of small businesses writing programs to do things that should really be left for people, calculators, or pencil and paper. New home computer owners spend hours using their computer to balance a checkbook that would normally take ten minutes without the computer. In terminal cases (pun intended), using the computer becomes an end in itself, and the owner sits in front of it continuously, day and night. Someone then has to be hired to run the business or support the family. Don't catch this disease. Run your spare-time business with your imagination, a pencil, and some paper. Maintain your perspective relative to how computers should and should not be used. If you suddenly realize that you are becoming preoccupied with using your computer instead of making money with it, pull the plug. You'll be amazed to discover that you can still function normally.

### Failure-Prone Behavior Patterns

You can be your own worst enemy when it comes to making money. Success involves conditioning yourself as well as finding good opportunities. Procrastination is the first enemy to be overcome. Maybe this book will convince you that making extra money in your spare time is possible. Maybe it will give you an idea for an article you think you could sell. Do you immediately start writing, or do you grab a beer and turn on the TV? You had a hard day at work or school, and next week is soon enough to get started. Unfortunately, next week you had a trip planned, and when you return you've sort of lost your enthusiasm for writing an article. Maybe you'll think of something easier if you wait a while. In the meantime there's another good show on TV, and tomorrow night there's a movie you'd like to see. We all tend to procrastinate. It's only a habit that you can break if you really want to. One trick involves rewarding yourself. Break work into small chunks. Do one chunk and reward yourself. Write the outline of your article first, then reward yourself with the beer and TV show.

We all know people who come up with a new get-rich-quick scheme every week. Some of these schemes even sound as though they might work. Unfortunately, these people spend hours talking about their ideas but never seem to get around to actually implementing them. This type of behavior is often blamed on laziness. It's also due to another factor you should be aware of. Talking about what you're doing can become a substitute for doing it. This factor is particularly troublesome for creative people such as artists, writers, and inventors. A lot of effort and time are usually needed to implement a new idea. These people have to be highly motivated to exert the required effort. A major motivation is the anticipation of favorable response to their work. If they explain what they are planning or describe the desired end result, they receive an immediate response. This can reduce their motivation to complete the work. Because they have already received a reaction, completion of the actual work seems less important. For this reason, successful writers, artists, and inventors are often reluctant to discuss their current projects in any detail. You have probably noticed this when watching TV interviews with creative people. You can learn a valuable lesson from them. If you are writing a new program, article, or book, don't talk about it until it's done. Otherwise, you may lose your incentive to finish it.

Optimism and pessimism must be carefully controlled. Too much pessimism can keep you from ever getting started in spare-time money-making activities. Overoptimism can be just as bad. Overoptimism about the size of your market or the time you will have to spend on a project can easily cause you to lose money instead of making it. Mail-order newcomers might see a magazine with a circulation of 500,000 and decide to advertise in it. They determine their product and advertising costs based on what they feel to be a conservative 10 per cent return and price the product accordingly. In actuality this is wildly optimistic. Fractional percentage returns from a single ad are considered good in the mail-order business. Such overoptimism results in losing money, and the newcomers conclude erroneously that no money can be made in mail-order sales. Always try to maintain a realistic outlook. Avoid excessive pessimism as well as overoptimism.

Before embarking on any spare-time money-making activity, evaluate your own personal characteristics, strengths, and weaknesses. Formal education and conventional wisdom stress the need for constant work on overcoming your weaknesses. This is nonsense. The end result of this approach is mediocrity. If you aren't born with natural musical ability, you can work on this weakness as hard as you want and never be a success. The person with natural ability who works just as hard on his or her strength will always beat you. Work on your weakness only to the point at which it no longer prevents you from capitalizing on your strengths. Emphasize the development of your natural abilities. Make sure that your money-making activity is compatible with your personality and abilities. You should already know if you're an extrovert or an introvert. Don't try direct sales or teaching if you are an introvert. Try to find money-making opportunities related to your existing hobbies. This will ensure that you'll enjoy what you're doing and that you can use existing skills. By all means avoid any activities you dislike. You will invariably fail and won't even have any fun in the process.

Learn to trust yourself. Develop your self-confidence and don't be afraid to trust your own judgment. You will then deserve full credit for any success and won't be able to blame somebody else for your failures. This builds character. Beware of experts who aren't rich. Free advice is generally worth less than you pay for it. Don't be afraid of failing. Many successful people learned most of what they needed to know for success from their own failures. Analyze the reasons for your failures and learn from them. Don't be stubborn and stick with a bad project just because it's your idea or because you hate to lose the time and money already invested in it. People have a tendency to avoid selling a stock that's going down in price because they don't want to take a small loss or admit they might have guessed wrong. They'd rather wait until they're sure they guessed wrong and take a big loss. The same mistake is often made with business ideas. At the same time, you shouldn't give up too soon on an idea you feel is right. The inventor of *Monopoly* succeeded by refusing to give up after his game was rejected by major companies. Here's where your judgment comes in. Always try to be objective. If your idea satisfies real needs, chances are you will sooner or later succeed with it.

## Luck Management and Synergy

Most success is due to luck. Some people are lucky enough to be born rich. Some are lucky enough to buy a winning lottery ticket or a stock that unpredictably doubles in the next three weeks. An obscure actress luckily gets a part in a TV series that is the surprise hit of the new season. A struggling writer is surprised when her new book becomes a best seller. The fact that success involves luck discourages most people. They don't realize that there are rules for luck management that can improve the chances for success.

Let's take a closer look at luck. It involves probabilities. The first rule of luck  management is easy. If you don't play the game, your probability of winning is zero. The lucky person who bought the winning lottery ticket had to go out and buy it. This gave him the edge over some-one who didn't exert this rather minor amount of effort. You can't get lucky and sell an article unless you write one. You can't find that great job if you're not looking. If you've decided to play the spare-time money-making game, you've already raised your odds of winning to something larger than zero per cent.

Another rule of luck management involves being in the right place at the right time. This further improves your chances for success. At this time the booming microcomputer industry is certainly the right place to find new spare-time money-making opportunities. New com-panies, publications, businesses, and products appear almost weekly. Several individuals have already made fortunes and have temporarily retired from active participation. Most of the really big action lies ahead. Watch trends and look for new specialized opportunities that can further improve your chances for success.

The next rule of luck management relates to gambling strategy. The successful gambler bets or plays only when he has an edge. Look for opportunities where you have an advantage over the competition. Local services, customized products, and small specialized markets provide opportunities where you have an advantage over large companies. Your imagination, special interests, or skills can give you an edge over compe-tition. Your own microcomputer and unique programs could give you an advantage in the areas of services or stock market speculation. If you don't feel that any of your abilities is unusual, look for combinations of interests or skills that might be unique. Always be looking for those op-portunities where you might have an advantage. Pursue such oppor-tunities when they occur because the odds of success are in your favor.

One more rule of luck management concerns your approach to making money. Doing your homework, paying attention to detail, and performing in a professional manner will improve your chances for suc-cess. An indifferent or sloppy approach will kill your chances.

Still another rule of luck management involves multiple bets. You will probably have a better chance to make money if you try a large number of simple, inexpensive approaches. Inventing is one illustration of this rule. The chances of selling a new game or toy to a major company is very small. The company may accept only one out of every thousand or more ideas submitted to them. If you do your homework and prepare a professional presentation, you might increase the odds of acceptance by a factor of ten. These are still bad odds for you. You will be able to improve the odds further by inventing ten games. This approach may actually improve the odds of selling any single game when companies realize that you're not a one-idea amateur. At least they'll become familiar with your name. Things like stock options and inventions are areas in which the potential payoff is so high you can afford a string of losses.

The last rule of luck management involves staying with a winning streak. Gamblers do this automatically. In the stock market, a price trend is more likely to continue than to reverse, so it seldom pays to bet against it. If you achieve success in some activity, it will usually pay to continue. For example, if you are successful in selling several articles, it will become easier to write and sell new ones. In the book field many publishers give top priority to manuscripts submitted by previously published authors and even solicit manuscripts from them. Success in a specific activity means that the odds favor your continued success. Never fight the odds when they're in your favor.

Synergy involves combinations of things. Many new ideas, inventions, and business opportunities involve combinations. Combining microcomputers and TV sets produced video games. Combining microcomputers and stock trading systems might provide you with an opportunity to become rich. Combining an interest in programming with experience as a high school teacher could provide an opportunity to become a highly paid educational consultant. Combining the clothespin principle with an electronic testing problem resulted in a new popular electronic tool. Look for new combinations of existing products, skills, businesses, marketing approaches, interests, and ideas. There's gold in them there combinations.

Don't forget to look for multiple applications of the same basic idea. Computer programs, articles, a best-selling plastic game, and a popular electronic toy have all been based on the single idea of guessing a hidden number. When you come up with an idea, try to think of all its possible applications. If you don't, somebody else will.

# 3

## Resources You Can Use

### Microcomputer Books

Learning as much as you can about microcomputers will increase your opportunities to make money. You can't creatively apply knowledge you don't have. Learning about computers and programming will be a continuing activity for you. New developments are almost weekly events in the rapidly changing microcomputer industry. Fortunately, you can obtain an excellent background in microcomputers and programming from books. Later on you will probably want to buy a home computer to obtain hands-on experience. You will also need a computer of your own to pursue many of the ideas in this book. Learning about computers comes first, however. Buying one can come later. This book even shows you ways to turn your new knowledge into money before you own a computer.

There are currently many good books on all aspects of microcomputers from beginning programming to advanced hardware design. You can find these books in your local library, bookstore, or computer store. Browsing through bookstores and libraries should become a regular habit for anyone seriously interested in making money. Computer books are also advertised in microcomputer magazines described in the next section. Several of these magazines also provide reviews of new microcomputer books.

Books are your best source of background knowledge. You should not depend on them for current information. By the time a book is written and published, information on specific products, prices, and trends is often out of date. Later on we discuss sources of current information.

You can even turn your book browsing into a search for money-making opportunities. As you look at computer books in stores, keep a list of their publishers. This tells you which publishers might be interested in your new book should you decide to write one. Writing a book is not

21

as impossible as it might seem. We discuss why in Chapter 5. When you see publishers that are selling their products in regular bookstores as well as computer stores and magazines, give them four stars on your list. They will probably provide you with the opportunity for maximum royalties on your book.

Book browsing can help you in another way. Keep a list of titles of all the books you see that are related to microcomputers. This will help tell you what kind of new book to write and what kind to avoid. Right now everyone seems to be writing general microcomputer beginner's books, how to program in BASIC books, and books on standard business applications of computers. Avoid types of books that appear to be overdone. Your chances of selling another one will be small unless you have a really new approach. Try to find gaps to fill. Look for needs not satisfied by existing books.

If you are a computer beginner, here are some books that can help you get started learning. They can be found in book or computer stores, or they can be ordered from ads in computer magazines. There are, of course, many other excellent beginner books available.

*The First Book of Microcomputers* by Robert Moody is published by the Hayden Book Company, Inc. It's a nice introduction to computers written in simple English. It explains many of the computer terms you should know.

*Beginner's Guide to Home Computers* by Marvin Grosswirth is published by Doubleday & Company, Inc. It is another easy beginner's book to start with.

*The Home Computer Book* by Len Buckwalter is published by Pocket Books, a Simon & Schuster Division of Gulf & Western Corp. It has lots of hardware photographs and provides a number of short programs written in BASIC.

*How to Profit from Your Personal Computer* by Ted Lewis is also published by Hayden Book Company. It is a well-written introduction to common business applications of computers.

*Basic BASIC* by James S. Coan is another Hayden book. It explains the most popular microcomputer language. It's got lots of examples related to mathematics. For easier BASIC books, check your local computer or Radio Shack store.

*CMOS Cookbook* by Don Lancaster is publisher by Howard W. Sams & Co., Inc. It is not a beginner's computer book. It is not even a computer book. It is a book for hardware hackers. If you are a hardware hacker, or want to be one, never miss a chance to read anything written by Don Lancaster.

Because new books are constantly being published, lengthy lists would be a waste of time here. Browsing through stores that carry computer books will quickly identify the ones that you'll need as you move up your personal learning curve.

## Computer Magazines

Magazines are the magic windows through which you can watch the constantly changing microcomputer industry. Next to your imagination, they represent your most valuable resource for making money. You should subscribe to as many as you can afford. In this section we discuss the most popular ones and what they can do for you.

Microcomputer magazines can keep you up to date on rumors, companies, people, and new products or services. They can educate you and stimulate your imagination. Always read magazines from cover to cover. Relative to making money, you can often learn more from advertisements than you can from articles. The ads are your guide to price, programming language, and application trends. Advertisements may even provide free market research. For example, a small ad that appears once or twice and then disappears could indicate the lack of a market for a product or service. One that continues to appear month after month could indicate a popular product or service.

Look at an advertisement carefully. Does it make you want to buy the product? If not, why? Can you rewrite the ad to make it better? If the answer to the last question is yes, maybe you should contact the company to see if they'll pay you to write better ads for them. In any case, you're getting a free lesson in advertising that will come in handy some day. While you're at it, start looking critically at TV commercials and ads in consumer magazines. You may be able to apply some of these successful approaches to your microcomputer money-making activities.

Many computer magazines pay for articles. Read the magazine to determine what types of articles they're interested in. Watch the editorials for clues to new types of articles they may be looking for. Editorials can also indicate what would appeal to a specific editor. Magazines need all types of articles and pay up to $50 per printed page for suitable material. Writing articles could easily pay for your first computer. Several magazines also publish books and programs which they then advertise for sale in the magazine.

Microcomputer magazines also provide you with a way to advertise your product or service nationally. Many individuals and companies depend on magazine advertising for a major part of their business. Local computer stores usually sell magazines so you can get an idea of which ones might appeal to you or your potential customers.

*Byte Magazine* is one of the most popular. It's published monthly by *Byte* Publications Inc., 70 Main St., Peterborough NH 03458. Its circulation is around 100,000. It buys over 200 articles per year from freelancers. It emphasizes personal computers for college-educated users. It appeals to intermediate or advanced programmers and hardware hackers.

*Creative Computing* was one of the first home computer magazines and is currently growing in popularity. Its circulation is about 50,000. The address is Box 789–M, Morristown, NJ 07960. It emphasizes the use of computers in homes and schools. It covers history, careers, simulations, puzzles, games, novel applications, and special purpose home microcomputers. It buys over 200 articles per year from freelancers in lengths from 500 to 3,000 words. It also publishes books, games, and programs.

*Kilobaud* is published monthly. The address is Peterborough NH 03458. It has a nice mixture of hardware and software articles appealing to a wide range of interests and abilities. It pays well for articles. *Kilobaud* also publishes programs for home and business applications on popular microcomputers such as the PET and TRS–80.

*Interface Age* is published monthly by McPheters, Wolfe & Jones, 16704 Marquardt Ave., Cerritos CA 90701. It seems to be aimed at intermediate and advanced programmers. Business applications are also stressed. It runs excellent surveys of available hardware.

*Personal Computing* is published monthly by Benwill Publishing Corp., 1050 Commonwealth Ave., Boston MA 02215. Its circulation is about 40,000. It is aimed at general personal computer interests. The magazine buys freelance articles on a wide range of computer subjects, including humorous fiction and money-making ideas. This is a good magazine for unusual application ideas.

*People's Computers* (or *Recreational Computing*) is published by People's Computer Company, 1263 El Camino Real, Box E, Menlo Park CA 94025. It doesn't run ads, pay for articles, or have a large circulation. It does, however, represent the views of very imaginative people who were pioneers in home computing. They deserve your financial support, and you'll be rewarded with lots of new ideas and perspectives on computers.

*Popular Electronics* is a gold mine of opportunities for hardware hackers. Its circulation is over 400,000, and it's available at most newsstands. They pay well for informational, how-to, and technical articles aimed at electronic experimenters, hi-fi buffs, and computer hobbyists. You should be an intermediate or advanced hardware hacker to write for this magazine, which is a source of parts, circuit ideas, and construction projects for all hardware hackers. It has published many pioneering microcomputer construction articles and runs a regular computer column.

*Elementary Electronics* is another magazine specializing in electronic construction projects. It's available at newsstands and has a circulation over 200,000. This magazine aims more at beginning hardware hackers.

*Radio Electronics* also publishes electronic construction articles and advertises parts and test equipment. It buys articles written from the viewpoint of the TV service technician or serious experimenter. It publishes some construction projects and tutorial material related to microcomputers. There is also a regular computer column.

Magazines change with time. They may decide to change their emphasis or style to attract more readers or different types of readers. A new editor can also result in a change in direction. You should continuously review all available magazines to determine their current value to you.

There are, of course, many other excellent computer-related magazines. They range from technical journals such as *The IEEE Transactions on Computers* to *Dr. Dobbs Journal of Computer Calisthenics & Orthodontia*. There are magazines for computer engineers, professional programmers, serious computer music students, and teachers. Most of these are aimed at very specialized interests and abilities.

## Stores, Clubs, User Groups, and Shows

Local microcomputer retail stores are relatively new. There are probably over a thousand spread around the country already, and new ones seem to be opening every day. They sell a wide range of general purpose microcomputers together with optional input-output devices such as printers and magnetic disc data storage units. They also stock microcomputer books, magazines, parts, programs, tools, test instruments, and accessories. Some also handle video games, calculators, and special purpose microcomputers such as chess playing machines. They serve local home, school, and business microcomputer users. Most of them emphasize small business applications and also function as consultants in this area.

By all means visit your local computer store often. You can see new hardware and books. A local store might provide part-time employment or consulting opportunities for you. They might need part-time programming or computer repair services. Spare-time teaching or selling opportunities may exist. They might even help you sell your product or services.

Over 5,000 Radio Shack stores exist. Most of them sell only the Radio Shack TRS–80 computer. They also sell a number of computer books and electronic parts. You should become familiar with Radio Shack because their computer is currently outselling most of the competition.

There are hundreds of local computer clubs in the country. They are often listed in microcomputer magazines. Such clubs are groups of individuals who own or who are interested in owning a low-cost computer. Club meetings provide an opportunity to meet other people with common interests, hear guest speakers, see computer demonstrations, swap hardware or software, and learn more about this fascinating new hobby. Members of such clubs usually represent a wide range of specialized interests and abilities. You should join a club if one exists in your area. It provides an excellent opportunity to learn about computers, discuss ideas, and make personal contacts that may be useful in the future.

Many larger clubs also publish monthly newsletters. Advertising rates are very low for these limited-circulation club publications. This provides you with an inexpensive way to test your market for a new product or service before spending lots of money for advertising in national magazines with large circulation. Club magazines are also a logical place to advertise local services such as kit building, customizing, repair, or programming.

Popular new computers form the basis of national user groups and newsletters. Each newsletter is concerned with providing information for owners of a specific computer. This information usually relates to modifications, programs, new applications, new attachments, tips on use, and anything else of interest to the owner of a specific computer. These newsletters are often published monthly and might be in the form of printed material, cassettes, or magnetic discs. Some newsletters will buy programs from you on an outright sale or royalty basis. Some will pay for articles of interest to their readers. Generally, the rate of pay is low. If you have a product, service, or program designed for a specific microcomputer, these newsletters or user group publications can be a good place to advertise. If you own a computer, you should belong to its major user group.

There are other types of user groups and newsletters that can be useful to you. These groups are based on a specialized application area such as music, medicine, gambling, stock market speculation, real estate investment, and the like. If you have a specialized interest, you might consider starting a newsletter. If you find an existing newsletter related to your specific interest, you might consider developing a new program or product to advertise in it.

Trade shows give you an opportunity for first-hand observation of new product trends. There are two major personal computer shows and a variety of smaller local shows each year. Personal computer exhibitions have also become a part of many professional engineering conventions. Personal computer shows are usually advertised or listed well ahead of time in the microcomputer magazines. Attending one of these shows gives you a chance to see most of the latest products. You can hear a variety of lectures by people active in the microcomputer industry. If you have your own product, a trade show provides a place to sell it or obtain customer reactions.

Computer stores, clubs, user groups, and trade shows can help you in a number of ways. New ones appear and old ones fade out of sight rapidly so it's impractical to list them in a book. Some people even make money by maintaining current lists. Magazines will help you keep up to date in these areas.

### Aids for Authors

Freelance writing provides spare-time income opportunities for beginners or experts. You don't even need a computer in many cases. Some specialized knowledge, a new idea, or just a fresh slant on an old subject can make you a successful writer. Chapter 5 gives you some help with what to write and where to sell it. This section guides you toward the background information required by all writers. Writing is an ideal spare-time activity. You can do it anywhere at any time. You can write on trips, during lunch, evenings, or on weekends without interfering with your full-time job.

If you are really serious about writing for money, a book entitled *1979 Writer's Market* will be your best friend. Published by Writer's Digest Books, 9933 Alliance Rd., Cincinnati OH 45242, it's available in most bookstores and libraries. It costs about $15. A new edition is published every year. It contains information on copyright, preparing manuscripts, submitting your work, and other subjects of interest to authors. The largest and most valuable part of the book is the section about where to sell your material. Thousands of book publishers, company publications, and magazines of all types are listed. Needs, prices paid, addresses, and names of editors are provided for each listing. There are a lot of listings. The current edition of this book runs to 900 pages. As a bonus you get names of cartoonists and greeting card publishers who will pay you for good ideas.

You can use this amazing book in several ways. Just looking at the size of the market for books and articles can give you an incentive to get out your pencil and paper. If you have a specific idea for an article or book, you can locate publishers who might be interested in it. Reading through the lists of trade publications and special interest magazines can trigger ideas for specialized microcomputer applications in various fields. The resulting program or article could make money for you.

The *Writer's Market* has been quite popular over the years. The following books are also available from the same publisher: *Artist's Market, Photographer's Market, Craftworker's Market,* and *Songwriter's Market.* You might find some useful ideas in these, too.

*Writer's Digest* is a monthly magazine you can find on most newsstands. It provides how-to articles on writing and short lists of markets. *The Writer* is another magazine of the same type that you may find useful. These magazines also advertise books on all aspects of writing. Some of these books can be extremely helpful for beginners. Others are useful for specific types of writing such as humor, fiction, or technical articles. Books on the business or legal aspects of writing are also available if you need them.

*Writing for the Markets* by David Raffelock is a good introduction to writing. It's published by Funk & Wagnalls. *How to Write Nonfiction That Sells* by F. A. Rockwell is another good how-to-write book. It's published by Contemporary Books, Inc., 180 N. Michigan Ave., Chicago IL 60601. *Advertising—How to Write the Kind That Works* is an excellent book written by David L. Malickson and John W. Nason and published by Charles Scribner's Sons, New York.

Visit your local bookstore or library to find books on the art of writing. Good, saleable writing requires practice. Books can help you with technique and motivation. They can teach you how to slant articles and start your creative juices flowing. Only hours of writing and rewriting will help you develop the required skill. Don't get discouraged initially. Tackle small projects first. You'll improve with practice and time.

# 4

# Choosing Your Hardware

## Plan Before You Buy

If you're a typical home computer hobbyist, you'll be anxious to buy a computer to play with as soon as possible. Chances are you'll buy the newest, most expensive model you can afford with as many options as possible. The last thing you'll worry about is what you can use it for. You'll be preoccupied with discussing features of different computers and programming languages outside the context of any specific application. Collecting hardware is an addiction with all types of hobbyists. There are do-it-yourself bugs with basement workshops full of the latest tools who may actually build only a picture frame or bookshelf every few years. There are hi-fi buffs with thousands of dollars worth of equipment who seldom listen to music except to demonstrate or test their hardware.

I have known people who buy an inexpensive computer and immediately begin expanding it. They add more memory and input-output devices. Then they start developing fancy operating systems or editing software. Then they add some more memory. At each step of the expansion process, they are convinced that any day now they will be ready to start actually using their system for something. For many that day will never come. There will always be something new to add first.

As a spare-time money maker, you can't afford to become addicted to buying and playing with hardware as an end in itself. Your time is valuable, and money is a scarce resource to be spent only after you have calculated the expected return. This doesn't mean that making money can't be fun. It can be more fun than going into debt or sacrificing future financial independence to achieve instant gratification Spare-time income building can permit you to buy even more expensive toys in the future.

Before buying hardware you should have a money-making plan that includes exactly what the hardware will be used for. You can then intelligently select the specific hardware you need without paying for unnecessary features or options. You may often find that to make money low-cost systems are better than higher priced ones. For example, suppose you want to develop programs for a large market. Wouldn't you suppose that most people will own the lowest cost version of a popular computer? People who have added costly options to their system should, of course, also be able to use your programs. Notice the different approaches. Typical hobbyists will want the fanciest version of a computer so they can do the maximum number of things with it whenever they decide what those things are. You will need only the lowest cost version because you know exactly what you want it for.

Don't be in any rush to buy hardware. It takes time to determine how popular a new computer will become. Knowing this is sometimes more important to you than what it does. Prices of new microcomputers are still dropping, so you don't have to rush out and buy before the price goes

**Fig. 1.** The TI-59 programmable calculator. (*Courtesy* Texas Instruments)

up, as with houses or cars. For some applications, used microcomputers or input-output devices may be adequate and save you money. If you develop a winning stock speculation system, do you really care about running it on a cheap used computer?

Remember that your initial money should be spent on books and magazines for educational purposes. Your time should be spent in learning about microcomputers, exercising your imagination, and planning. You may find yourself in the same position as many companies that study the applications of computers in their business. The study itself shows how efficiency can be improved without buying a computer. You, too, can use your knowledge of computers to make money without owning a computer.

Sooner or later you will probably want to buy hardware to expand your opportunities. The following sections describe various types of microcomputers available now and discuss what the future may bring. Just remember that hardware popularity changes rapidly as new computers appear, and predictions of the future are notoriously unreliable—no matter who makes them. The highly competitive microcomputer industry is like a soap opera. You'll just have to tune in every day to see what's new and who's doing what to whom.

Descriptions of available hardware are kept brief because this is primarily a money-making idea book. They are included only to give you some idea of what's available. Discussion is also limited to typical general purpose microcomputers.

## Programmable Calculators

The TI–59 by Texas Instruments is a typical example of a programmable calculator that is actually a general purpose microcomputer. Add a PC–100A printer and you've got a complete system with hard copy output for $400 or less. For many mathematical applications this system can't be beat. A relatively small internal memory for data and programs is provided. You can expand the program memory by plugging in small, optional Read Only Memory (ROM) modules containing specialized programs or subroutines. A number of these specialized modules are available, including ones for statistics and navigation applications.

External data and program storage consists of small magnetic strips. You can write a program and record it on one of these magnetic strips for subsequent use. A number of programs are available in this form for users. The calculator itself runs on batteries and will fit in a pocket or purse. With the printer it's easily carried in a briefcase, which makes it handy for on-the-road use by salesmen, engineers, or gamblers.

The TI–59 type of microcomputer is perfect for applications involving lengthy or complex calculations with relatively small amounts of numerical input data. Programs for evaluating stock option prices have been offered for sale in financial publications. There is a user group for program exchange. Programs involving gambling systems have appeared for sale by individuals. Programs related to football, baseball, or race handicapping have appeared in various gambling publications. A random number generator permits the user to simulate and test betting systems for blackjack, craps, baccarat, and other games.

Although programmable calculators are limited to certain types of applications, they do represent one form of low-cost, general purpose microcomputer suitable for home or business use.

**Fig. 2.** CSC LM-1 Logic Monitor. (*Courtesy* Continental Specialites Corp.)

## Single Card Computers

Single card computers were the first type of general purpose microcomputer available for hobby use. They were originally developed to give engineers hands-on experience with microcomputer chips of various types at minimum cost. Many of the first products of this class were offered in kit form. They consist of a single printed circuit card containing a complete general purpose microcomputer with limited input-output and memory capabilities. Provisions are usually made for adding input-output devices and extra memory. Single card computers are usually naked computers with all parts hanging out in plain sight. Fancy cabinets cost extra money.

If you're a potential hardware hacker, these single card microcomputers can get you involved at minimum cost. Several have first appeared as construction projects in electronics magazines. You can use

**Fig. 3.** The KIM-1 single card microcomputer. (*Courtesy* Commodore Business Machines, Inc.)

them to experiment with new input-output attachments and machine language programs. They can provide the basis for customized controllers or special purpose systems. There are a number of single card systems available. Prices generally range from $150 to $400. For most of them, you will have to add at least the cost of an audio cassette recorder for external data or program storage. Three such microcomputers are described here to give you an idea of what's available.

The KIM-1 by Mos Technology (a division of Commodore Business Machines, Inc.) was one of the most popular single card microcomputers. It currently sells for less than $200. It includes 1,000 bytes of user memory, a small keyboard, and a six-digit display similar to the type seen on calculators. You can add a standard audio cassette recorder to save data and programs for later use. It has fifteen lines for input-output expansion. Because it was one of the lowest cost units available at the time of its introduction, it became very popular. This popularity resulted in the appearance of books, articles, newsletters, and attachments for it. There are large numbers of this microcomputer in use, and it's still being sold.

A newer single card microcomputer is the COSMAC VIP by RCA. It sells for about $250 and is similar to the KIM–1. The COSMAC VIP, however, provides 2,000 bytes of memory and has a novel user language called CHIP–8. The most interesting feature is the inclusion of a video graphic display capability. Adding a TV set or video monitor permits its use for video games or advertising displays.

Another new single card microcomputer is the AIM 65 by Rockwell International. This unit sells for $375. It includes a full keyboard similar to a typewriter and a twenty-column printer. The full keyboard and printer might be useful in a number of applications, such as factory testing and stock price analysis.

Look at single card microcomputers if you are interested in learning about hardware details or have a customized system in mind. They

**Fig. 4.** The COSMAC VIP with user-supplied video monitor and audio cassette tape recorder. (*Courtesy* RCA Corp.)

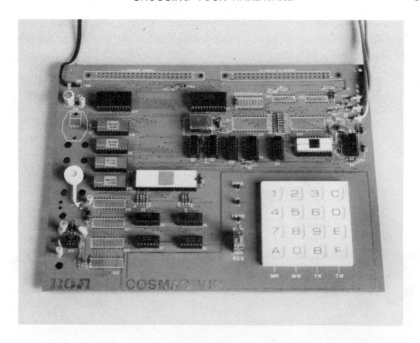

**Fig. 5.** The COSMAC VIP. (*Courtesy* RCA Corp.)

make excellent controllers for other devices. They generally have a limited market relative to microcomputers that are packaged attractively, and are easier to use.

## Complete Systems

Low-cost, attractively packaged, easy-to-use, ready-to-run, general purpose microcomputers are currently getting a lot of attention. Three typical products are described here. There are many others, and many new ones can be expected. The prices mentioned relate to minimum system configurations. Adding various memory and input-output options can push the price of these computers up into the $2,000 to $4,000 range.

**Fig. 6.** The AIM 65 microcomputer. (*Courtesy* Rockwell International)

The APPLE II by Apple Computer, Inc. is a popular microcomputer sold in most computer stores. A minimum system is priced under $1,000. This computer started out as a single card hobby type and evolved into its present, nicely packaged form. It is the only one of the three computers discussed here that offers a color TV display capability. This feature and its wide availability in computer stores gives it a special appeal to home users. The availability of video game programs and optional joystick playing controls reinforces this home use appeal. The manufacturer also offers a series of stock market programs. With extra-cost hardware, you can feed these programs with up-to-date stock market data via your telephone. A fancy version of BASIC comes with this computer.

The PET by Commodore Business Machines is priced at about $800. This computer, including a nine-inch black and white TV screen display, keyboard, and cassette recorder, is contained in a single, attractive, plastic cabinet that can sit on a table or desk. It has a nice graphics capability and includes a fancy version of BASIC for programming. It is interesting because it was produced by a large company and aimed

**Fig. 7.** The Apple II system. (*Courtesy* Apple Computer Inc.)

**Fig. 8.** The PET 2001 series personal computer. (*Courtesy* Commodore Business Machines, Inc.)

initially at the home computer market. It has attracted a large following. Independent newsletter and software publishers are jumping into the market with products designed for the PET.

The TRS–80 by Radio Shack may be the most interesting current microcomputer system. It's only sold through Radio Shack stores, but there are well over 5,000 of these stores in the country. It sells for $500 in its smallest form and includes a simplified version of BASIC that is easy to learn and adequate for a wide range of applications. It has medium resolution graphics capability. It's packaged in three parts. The computer and keyboard are provided in a separate cabinet. A twelve-inch black and white TV display and an audio cassette recorder are attached to the computer module with plug-in cables. This modular construction is actually an advantage in many cases. It makes the system extremely portable. The cassette recorder and TV display are easily replaced or repaired if required.

The TRS–80 currently has several potential advantages over other computers in the area of spare-time money-making opportunities. High volume is its first advantage. Although sales figures are not generally available, the TRS–80 is probably outselling most other computers. It has been estimated that as many as 100,000 TRS–80 computers have been sold. This computer is certainly generating a large need for new applications, programs, and attachments. Low cost is a second advantage of the TRS–80. Its modular construction lets you buy a spare computer for as little as $400 if you already own a cassette recorder and video monitor. If you are providing a computer service, renting computers, playing the stock mar-

**Fig. 9.** The TRS-80 computer. (*Courtesy* Radio Shack)

ket, or if you are dependent on your computer for any other reason, having a spare could be important. Modularity provides another important advantage in some applications. You can easily replace the twelve-inch TV monitor with a unit with a larger screen size for demonstration, teaching, or advertising display applications.

Nobody is sure what the future will hold. Right now, however, I lean toward the TRS-80 as being the most useful machine for many spare-time money-making activities. This doesn't mean that there aren't better choices for specific applications. That's why it's so important for you to plan your money-making activity in detail before rushing out to buy any hardware. Then you won't get bogged down comparing features. You can look for the lowest cost computer that is adequate for your specific purposes.

**Fig. 10.** The TRS-80 Model II microcomputer. (*Courtesy* Radio Shack)

### Input-Output Options

Now that you have some idea of what types of minimum cost, general purpose microcomputers are available, we'll discuss some of the types of optional equipment available. These options can enhance the capabilities of your computer but will also push the cost up.

In most minimum-cost computers a standard audio cassette recorder provides external data and program storage capability. A minimum-cost TRS-80 computer can be used to calculate stock price moving averages. Average weekly stock prices for a specific stock are stored on a cassette. After loading the appropriate program from another cassette, the stock price tape is read in. You can then enter the period for which you want the moving average calculated, and the computer displays the result in the form of a graph or table on the TV screen. With audio cassettes, reading in the program and 200 average stock prices can take as long as five minutes. Adding a magnetic disc storage unit can reduce this time to several seconds and add about $1,000 to the cost of your original $500 system.

**Fig. 11.** A magnified photograph of integrated circuit chips. (*Courtesy* Rockwell International)

Although relatively slow magnetic tape cassettes are adequate for many applications, they are impractical for others. If you need fast random access to large files of data such as customer records, product inventory, or information on specific subjects, a magnetic disc device may be required. There are several units available for microcomputers. They will add $500 to $1,000 to the cost of your system.

Many applications of computers need printed output. Adding a printer to your computer can cost several hundred to several thousand dollars. If you need nice looking typewriter quality printing, with upper and lower case letters, figure on spending at least $2,000 extra for new equipment. Used, high-quality printing devices might be obtained for $1,000. You might obtain low-quality printing on paper tape rolls similar to those used on cash registers for as low as several hundred dollars.

If you want a plotter for producing graphs and computer artwork, you can plan on spending at least $1,000. High-resolution color TV display will cost you more than simple black and white. You can obtain devices to permit your computer to send or receive data over the telephone at extra cost, of course. You can add joysticks for playing games or remote control devices that let your computer turn your house lights on and off. Just look through computer magazines and books to see all the attachments available for your computer. Maybe you'll be able to invent some new ones.

You must read ads for computers carefully. Some microcomputer companies have a cute trick of discussing the minimum system price together with applications of expanded systems that cost two or three times as much as the minimum system. They also like to mention a variety of possible applications without mentioning that appropriate software isn't available yet. Always read computer ads carefully to determine exactly what is, and what isn't, included in the specified price. The applications of computers aren't limited by your imagination as much as by the price of hardware.

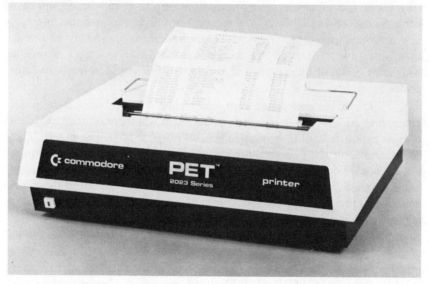

**Fig. 12.** The PET 2023 series printer. (*Courtesy* Commodore Business Machines, Inc.)

**Fig. 13.** The Turtle by Terrapin, Inc., is an electronic home robot controllable by microprocessor.

### Keep One Eye on the Future

Prices of small business-oriented microcomputers will probably stay about the same for a long time The emphasis will be on improved performance and reliability. The reason for this is the fact that plenty of new microcomputer customers exist at present prices. Many companies have also underestimated the educational and service costs associated with sales to small businesses and will have to reflect these costs in future prices.

The lower cost home computer action will probably shift over to companies currently making video games, who will increase the capabilities of their products until they become general purpose home computers. These companies have the mass production and distribution capabilities required for the home computer market. Easier programming, new applications, and lower cost attachments are the primary needs in this segment of the micro-computer industry. Application emphasis should expand in the areas of education, music synthesis, and health. The eventual combination of micro-computers and videodisc technology can be expected. Home computers with arms or other mechanical attachments will evolve.

Look for increasing use of flat panel and single line alphanumeric displays instead of TV screens. You can expect new lower cost external data and program storage devices, which might include new magnetic disc, card, or strip devices. New all-electronic storage modules should eventually appear. The trend toward special purpose microcomputers in the form of toys, games, and household appliances should continue. You can probably expect computerized door chimes, can openers, and hair dryers.

The important thing to remember is that you're currently seeing the beginning of a new era in electronics. Many new products and money-making opportunities will continuously appear. You should be preparing yourself to take advantage of them as they occur.

**Fig. 14.** The 8748 microcomputer is a member of the MCS 48 single chip microcomputer family and includes an 8K EPROM and 27 I/0 on one chip. (*Courtesy* Intel Corp.)

# 5

# Writing for Money

## Nontechnical Articles

You have probably seen nontechnical articles on computers in popular magazines or Sunday newspaper supplements. These articles describe microcomputers in terms anyone can understand. They tell about new microcomputer products or what a computer is. They tell how low-cost microcomputers relate to reader's lives, hobbies, or jobs. They tell funny computer stories or tales of computer mistakes. Authors tell about personal experiences with computers or about their visit to a home computer show. They make readers afraid of computers, more comfortable with computers, or more interested in computers. Read some of them and you'll discover that sometimes the author knows less about computers than you do. Why shouldn't you get paid for writing this type of article? Maybe because you didn't recognize this computer-related money-making opportunity. You don't have to be a computer expert or own a computer to make money writing articles about computers.

You do need a pencil, some paper, a reasonable command of the English language, and ideas. You may already have the first two requirements. The third can be developed with the aid of some books on writing. This book tries to help you get started in coming up with ideas. A little knowledge about computers, a little research, the right slant, a catchy title, and several thousand words can earn you some extra money. Your copy of *Writer's Market* will provide you with the names of hundreds of magazines that might be interested in paying for your microcomputer articles.

Now for some ideas. You could base an article on one of the following titles:

Invite a Computer to Your Next Party
Giant Brains are Getting Smaller
Give Your Child a Computer This Christmas
Beat the Stock Market with Your Own Computer

Living with a Computer
Living with a Computer Nut
Why My Computer Hates Me
Dick and Jane Meet the Home Computer
Turn Your TV Set into a Computer
Make Old Age Fun . . . Get a Computer
New Home Computer Inventions Needed
Earn Extra Money with Your Own Computer
How Home Computers Can Help You Beat Inflation

Some of these titles may have already been used, but you should be able to think of lots of others. What other people are doing can make money for you. How about interviews with the owner of your local computer store or people using home computers in interesting ways? Can you find someone controlling Christmas lighting with a computer or making money with a home computer? Are microcomputers being used for educational purposes in a local school? How are inexpensive computers being used in research or in helping handicapped people? How about special education? What amazing new computer games, toys, or hi-fi equipment is available? Did you know that many new cars will have microcomputers built into them? How about computer control of new homes? All these subjects can provide article ideas for you. Photographs can also help sell articles.

Get out your *Writer's Market* book again. Look at all those company, trade, and special interest publications that pay for articles. Home computers related to gambling, hobbies, and music provide article possibilities. How teachers and parents can use home computers should be interesting. An article describing how a local toy store uses a small computer to improve business might appeal to one of the toy trade magazines. How churches and fraternal organizations can, or are, using inexpensive computers should have saleable article possibilities. Women's magazines might be interested in small computers and astrology. Men's magazines could be interested in how to liven up parties with a home computer or how one can be used to handicap football games.

You can even consider selling nontechnical articles to some of the computer magazines. Such articles would involve the history of microcomputers, or they could be interviews with microcomputer pioneers. Descriptions of novel applications or systems might also appeal to some computer magazines.

By now you should be thinking of even more ideas. Get out your pencil and write them down before you forget them. During the day, whenever you see or think of something that might provide the basis for an article, write it down. Keep a pencil and paper next to your bed at night. Some of your best ideas can come right before you fall asleep. If you don't sleep alone, explain your eccentric behavior by mentioning that you want to take notes on your dreams. You're on your way to becoming an author. Rewrite your first attempts at articles several times before you submit them to a publisher. Don't worry about your first fifty rejection slips; they're par for the course. In the next section we discuss some more types of nontechnical writing that can earn you even more money.

### Fillers and Fiction

Here are more ideas that don't require much technical background. They do require a sense of humor or some literary ability. If you are a programmer or engineer, you might as well skip this section.

There is a small market for computer-related cartoons, puzzles, greeting cards, poetry, humor, and fiction. Look through the microcomputer magazines to see which ones run this type of material. Your copy of *Writer's Market* will give you names of cartoonists and greeting card publishers who are looking for ideas. It will also tell you in what form to submit your ideas. You don't have to limit yourself to computer magazines. The increasing public interest in computers makes most magazines potential markets for this type of material. For special interest magazines, slant your computer humor accordingly. Several years ago I sold a fifteen-word idea for a computer greeting card for $50. This wasn't a lot of money, but it worked out to $100 an hour or $3.33 per word. It would have also paid for four microcomputer magazine subscriptions.

Short reviews of new microcomputer products are also bought by some consumer magazines. Photographs will help in this area. Short reviews of new microcomputer toys or games fit into this catagory. Look through your *Writer's Market* to find out who buys short items about new products.

Both consumer publications and microcomputer magazines could be markets for well-researched comparison guides on current products. Around Christmas many magazines like to provide comparisons of video games, home computers, or electronic toys for their readers. Microcomputer and electronic magazines frequently run comparison guides on hardware.

Novel electronic, computer, or programming tests might appeal to some magazines. These test the readers' knowledge in a specific area. Cute electronic, logic, or program puzzles could also earn you a few extra dollars from appropriate magazines.

If you like games and puzzles in general, you may be interested in subscribing to *Games*. This magazine is published bi-monthly by Games Publications, Inc., 515 Madison Ave., New York, NY 10022. A subscription costs $7.00 from *Games,* P.O. Box 10145, Des Moines, IA 50340. The magazine has new games and puzzles as well as interesting articles in each issue. It might give you an idea for a new game, puzzle, or computer program. It might also buy a game article from you.

### Information and Guides

Now that you've learned how to be a successful writer, maybe you're ready to become a publisher. You can publish your own material or get someone with a more technical background to write material for you. You can run your publishing empire from your kitchen table in your spare time. Rent a post office box, choose a company name, and promote yourself to president. You might not make a lot of money at first but think of the prestige. All you need is something to publish.

Hundreds of people successfully sell all sorts of printed information through the mail. This information ranges from "How to Make Wine in Your Bathtub" to the "Secret of Getting Rich for only $50." The secret of getting rich, by the way, usually involves selling the "Secret of Getting Rich" to other people for $50. The cost of having this information printed up at your local fast printing shop is negligible. It usually takes the form of several typewritten pages stapled together. If you want to get fancy, you can have the pages folded in half and stapled in the center to make a booklet. The minimum price you should charge is enough to cover your cost of printing, advertising, and mailing. The maximum price you can charge is what your customers are likely to think the information is worth to them. This opinion will be influenced by how you write your advertisement. I have seen cases where the effort that went into writing the ad obviously exceeded that which was devoted to preparing the information being sold. Since you don't want to become known in the trade as a fast-buck operator, you should give some thought to having information of real value to sell.

Your major contribution to this spare-time money-making activity will be the idea, the advertising, and order filling. If you lack the expertise required to prepare the information, find someone to write it for you on a royalty, partnership, or outright purchase basis. Let's look at some types of information involving microcomputers that people might be willing to buy from you. Make sure that someone else isn't already providing it before proceeding. The best way to check is by reading the ads in microcomputer magazines. Don't forget to read the classified ads in magazines that carry them. These are a favorite place to sell information. You might also consider direct mail selling, which involves sending advertising letters to a list of people who would be likely customers. There are even people who make their money by selling these lists. Direct mail selling is usually too expensive to be practical for low-cost information. If your information would appeal to owners of a specific microcomputer, you could advertise it in newsletters serving these owners.

A microcomputer author's guide might sell. It could provide information on what to write, where to sell it, and rates of pay. A bibliography of stock market or gambling systems might appeal to programmers. You could include a brief description of each system and whether or not computer implementation would be appropriate. A guide to available articles, books, and hardware related to computer music synthesis might sell. A home computer inventor's guide or instructions for converting a popular video game into a home computer could make money for you. Ideas for science experiments or using microcomputers in classrooms might have enough appeal to be profitable.

Up-to-date shoppers' guides to hardware or software could be general or specific in nature. Guides to software for specific computers should become popular as the number of independent software publishers increases. Specific instructions for making money with home computers should gain in popularity as more people become owners. Guides to articles, books, and attachments for specific computers are useful. Inexpensive home study courses in hardware or software could fill a need if well done. Information on using a microcomputer as a test instrument could appeal to electronic experimenters and hi-fi buffs. Detailed construction plans for novel cabinets or inexpensive machine language trainers might be considered.

You should have no trouble thinking up other ideas for information you can sell through the mail. Looking through magazines should give you even more ideas in this area. Don't forget that you can also sell this information in the form of cassettes that display the information on the screen of the customer's computer. The novelty value might help sell the information. This approach is feasible only when the information would appeal to owners of a specific microcomputer.

Selling information can also involve the business segment of the microcomputer industry. In general, you will have to be familiar with the specific area involved to be successful. You could, of course, team up with a doctor, car dealer, or real estate agent to develop microcomputer-related information of interest to these specialized fields.

## Books

If being the president of your own publishing empire doesn't appeal to you, maybe you should consider writing a book. This isn't as ridiculous an idea as it might sound at first. It's nice to believe that only experts write books, but many times it works in reverse. People become experts by writing books. Another factor in your favor is that the microcomputer industry is new and changing rapidly, so experts are hard to find. Despite this lack of experts, somebody still has to write books to keep the publishing business healthy.

Many microcomputer or programming books for beginners are written by people learning about computers. They take advantage of the research required to learn. Writing a book is like writing a program or teaching a course. It forces you to learn the subject. As new languages become popular, you could consider writing books for beginners. Sometimes a new or novel approach to teaching existing material can result in a book.

If you become involved in a new area of microcomputer use, you may discover that you have become an expert. One young author has written a book based on his design and construction of a simple home robot controlled by a microcomputer. There is still room for new home computer experts in the areas of music synthesis, health applications, handicapping systems, stock market systems, education, science experiments, dynamic optical illusions, occult sciences, parapsychology experimentation, model railroad control, photography, inventing, and creative thinking. If you have a hobby, you can become an expert at combining it with microcomputers.

Books that provide information on a specific computer are possible. You could include programs, attachments, programming techniques, and modifications. You should always obtain permission to use previously published material in a book of this type, and you should credit your sources. There are also books of useful subroutines for programmers. Books providing background information in a specific area would be useful for programmers. This background information could include reviews of the math involved in navigation, real estate management, surveying, sports handicapping, option pricing, astrology, amateur radio, or risk management. There are still lots of unfilled needs for books on home computers. Future needs will relate more to applications than to learning about hardware and programming.

This book is an idea book. It provides you with background, inspiration, and lots of ideas in the area of making money with home computers. It presents an overview of a large subject area. As a result, discussions of individual money-making activities are brief so that a variety of different activities can be covered. Many of these money-making approaches could be the subject of an entire book by themselves. If you successfully pursue one of these money-making activities, you should consider writing a book on it. Making extra money seems to be a universal desire. It should become a popular home computer application. Books on specific money-making approaches will always be in demand.

Other types of computer books that appear from time to time include ones on computer fraud, computer intelligence, computer humor, computer fiction, and even collections of computer art or cartoons. Books on computer trivia, computer history, and computer philosophy might sell. There don't appear to be many microcomputer books that really simplify computers and programming for the general public. Most books for beginners are aimed at teaching detailed fundamentals to future computer owners.

Spend as much time in bookstores and libraries as possible. Look through the wide variety of nonfiction and novelty books. Could you use any of these approaches in a book related to microcomputers? Could you combine microcomputers with the subject matter of any of these other books?

Writing a book is a major undertaking. You should plan on a minimum of 200 double-spaced typed pages. After picking your subject and doing your research, prepare an outline in the form of a table of contents. Break each chapter into smaller sections. Make rough notes about what you will say in each section. This will give you an idea of whether or not you have enough material for a book. If you don't, consider writing an article on your subject instead. If the book looks good at the outline stage, pick a preliminary title and write the first few chapters. If all looks well at this stage and you like the way it is going, start to query publishers for possible interest. If you get a positive response, submit the table of contents and several chapters. Proceed to finish the book; you may be on your way to a sale. Don't be overly optimistic about making a fortune on microcomputer book royalties. A good return would be $4,000 to $5,000 over several years; less could be expected. It's unlikely that anyone will want movie rights to a microcomputer book or that it will hit the best seller list unless you're clever enough to write pornographic microcomputer fiction. A book might pay for your home computer with a little extra to spare. Having your name on a book helps your ego and can also help smooth the way for additional writing activities.

### Pencil for Hire

You should always be working to improve your writing ability. It can help you in a variety of ways, and it's difficult to think of any examples where the ability to write well could hurt you. The ability to express your thoughts clearly in writing will be helpful in many full-time jobs and opens the door to a number of freelance writing opportunities.

This section discusses even more ways to turn your writing ability into spare-time cash.

In the previous section you were told that you didn't have to be an expert to write a book. Of course, if you are an expert it would help a lot. Suppose, however, that you can find a real expert who can't or doesn't want to write a book. This expert might be willing to pay you to write the book for her or share the royalties with you. Ghost writing and collaboration aren't new ideas in the writing field. They could provide money-making opportunities for you. It will help if you have previous writing experience although this may not be absolutely necessary. How do you find willing experts? You might meet someone with expertise at a computer club meeting. You could place an advertisement in computer or electronic magazines offering your writing services. If you see an article by someone who appears to be a technical expert in a specific area but a lousy writer, you might send a letter offering to collaborate on a book idea. Explain how you could do most of the tedious, time-consuming work involved in writing a book, including typing and proofreading. The person may say no, but you haven't lost anything by trying. He may even change his mind later. Collaborating with a highly skilled hardware hacker or programmer would be your best bet. Such a person can provide detailed hardware designs or programs, and you can build the rest of the book around his designs.

You could work this idea in reverse. You might have an idea for a microcomputer application book but no programming ability. You could specify the programs you need and find a programmer to write them for you. He would get a share of future royalties for his efforts. This collaboration approach can also be applied to articles for which you supply the idea and prepare the article while a hardware or software specialist works out the details you need.

Manufacturers need instruction manuals for products. You might offer to write manuals for smaller companies. If you see products that have terrible instruction manuals, write the company and offer to prepare a better one. Your first attempts could be done on an approval or speculation basis. Later on, when you have samples of your work, you can negotiate a price ahead of time. You might also consider writing advertisements or sales literature for smaller companies that seem to be weak in these areas.

Some publishers might pay you to edit or proofread book manuscripts. Some magazines use freelance associate editors for specific writing, editing, or review assignments. Program publishers might be interested in having good documentation prepared for programs. One major microcomputer company recently asked for help from outside writers to prepare users' manuals for programs they wanted to sell. If you have artistic ability, there are freelance opportunities to illustrate books, articles, and sales literature. I needed some humorous computer illustrations several years ago and found that many freelance commercial artists weren't even sure what computers looked like. If you're planning to attend a microcomputer trade show, you might try to get an assignment to cover it for a magazine. You will need to be a photographer as well as a writer for this type of work.

### Tutorials and Testimonials

If you are among the first owners of a new hardware product, many microcomputer magazine readers will be interested in your experience with it and an unbiased evaluation of it. If you read microcomputer magazines, you'll see this type of article once in a while. In the early days it was hard to avoid seeing articles describing the trials and tribulations of some author in his attempt to assemble a computer kit and get it working. As assembled and ready-to-run products became popular, this type of article appeared less often. When a new microcomputer appears, you'll still see lots of articles providing user opinions of it.

Another type of article you can write involves comparisons of different microcomputers and programming languages. Such articles can be a general comparison of features, or they can be related to performance. In the latter case, you might compare the performance of different microcomputers or languages relative to the same application. It pays to keep the application simple and be prepared for complaints from the losers.

Many microcomputer magazines try to satisfy both beginning and advanced readers. While older readers become less interested in computer basics, new readers are generally still beginners. As a result of new people entering the field, many magazines continue to run material for beginners. Tutorial articles on computer fundamentals can involve hardware or programming. Try to avoid duplicating existing articles. Look for a fresh slant or new approach to presenting tutorial material if you want to sell it. Look for novel teaching methods.

### Software Articles

Articles on software have two requirements. You need an interesting idea and a detailed program to implement it. This means you should have access to a microcomputer to write this type of article because you will have to design and debug your program. You might also have to provide a printed copy of your program. Some magazines might be willing to print your program from a cassette that you provide. Better check with the magazine to find out their specific requirements. You will probably have a better chance of selling a software article if it's based on a microcomputer that is popular with readers of the magazine.

You will also have to decide whether your program idea should be developed as an article for a magazine or as a program to be sold directly to users. The latter method of selling programs is discussed in Chapter 6. It is usually the most profitable approach if your program fills a widespread need. Program publishers generally don't want programs that have been published previously as magazine articles. The exception might be magazines that also publish programs for sale. Check with these magazines to find but what their policy is.

In general your approach to deciding what to do with an idea for a program involves several steps. A short, simple program is probably suitable for an article in a newsletter or magazine. If it's designed to illustrate some aspect of using a specific microcomputer or programming technique, it is also suited to an article. If the program is related to some specialized hardware attachment or computer modification, it should be developed in article form. If your program is large and seems to fill a widespread need, think in terms of direct sale of the final program to users.

Look through the microcomputer magazines to see what the current trends in software articles are. Seeing existing software articles will sometimes trigger an idea for a new one. Simple programs for novel games, puzzles, ESP testing, experiments, sound effects, seasonal graphics, animation, poetry composition, simulations, and demonstrations can make interesting articles. Simple interfaces and programs that permit microcomputers to be used in other hobbies are always popular. Applications of microcomputers to model railroading, ham radio, photography, greenhouse control, gardening, hi-fi, electronic experimenting, model rocketry, radio control, light shows, robots, and raising tropical fish could provide saleable article ideas.

Other software articles can involve education. Simple programs that illustrate the use of new language would fall into this category. Useful subroutines for programmers and how to use machine language are possible subjects for articles. Educational simulation of simplified tutorial or specialized computers is a currently neglected area. Software for use with new input-output devices is always needed. Educational programs of various types for children are always good material for articles.

Another area for software articles is that of programming aids. These include operating systems and editing systems to make programming faster or easier. You might even design very simple new interpretive languages for experimental use. Articles on test and diagnostic programs for microcomputers, memories, cassettes, discs, and input-output devices would fill an existing need.

Simple interfacing and software that permits direct communication between two or more computers is another interesting application area. This would permit games using multiple TV screens to be designed. "My computer can beat your computer" type games can also be developed. Activities involving telephone access to microcomputers should become increasingly popular.

As you become more involved with your home computer, you should be able to come up with a variety of ideas for software articles. For a good article, however, you'll need more than just a good idea. You have to slant your idea so that it appeals to the widest possible group of readers and dress it up so that it holds their interest. You should tell them what the program does for them and provide a clear description of how it works. Articles of this type are always needed and can earn you several hundred dollars each. They can provide you with valuable writing experience and contacts with magazine editors. Being a published author can enhance your prestige and help establish you as an expert in a specialized field. I have made a number of useful contacts in the microcomputer industry through letters received after publication of my articles. Articles might even result in future consulting, book review, associate editor, or column-writing opportunities.

Never submit an article to more than one magazine at a time. If you are impatient, write several articles to submit to different magazines. You can write and ask about your article if you have not heard from the publisher after six weeks. When you submit an article, always include a cover letter explaining why you think the article is right for the readers of this specific magazine. Keep your letter brief. If your background makes you particularly qualified to write the article, tell the editor why. Remember that when you sell an article you have lost all rights to the material. In some cases you can get your rights to subsequent use of the material back from the magazine publisher. If you anticipate doing this, make it a condition of the sale.

## Algorithms and Applications

You have probably seen many articles about algorithms and applications in microcomputer magazines. They fall between software articles and construction articles. They don't provide ready-to-run programs or detailed hardware construction plans. One type provides partially worked out application or device ideas. Another type provides background information about a specific microcomputer application area. Such articles are basically idea articles. In some cases you don't need a computer to write them, but you *will* need new ideas and research to be successful in this area.

Home computer owners have a wide variety of interests. They are always looking for new ideas for things to do with their computers. Many people enjoy writing their own programs but need new ideas for programs they can develop. Many advanced hardware hackers are also looking for new projects to work on. You can satisfy these needs for new ideas and earn extra money at the same time. Programmers and hardware hackers are specialists. They have very specific skills that have a potentially wide area of application. Unfortunately, most of them know very little about most of these potential areas of application but are anxious to learn. Here's where you come in by supplying background information on areas in which microcomputers might be used.

Home microcomputers are ideal for sports handicapping or stock market trading. How many owners know very much about either area? Here's your chance to research and write about specific handicapping systems or stock trading systems that lend themselves to home computer implementation. Limit your article to one or two systems and describe the theory as well as the math involved. Include some examples of how the system works on real data. You aren't writing a book so you don't have to cover the entire field in one article.

There are excellent home computer applications in the areas of real estate investing, risk management, and aids for the handicapped. Why not do some homework and write some stimulating background articles in these areas? Do you have some novel ideas for home security, holiday displays, music synthesis, or impressive home computer demonstrations? Turn your ideas into articles

Background information on software techniques for animation, data file organization, random number generation, motion simulation, statistical calculations, graph plotting, and picture drawing can provide the basis for new articles. New programming approaches, such as *structured, fill in the blank,* or *question and answer* types, provide additional article material. Articles on random variables, Monte Carlo, linear programming, game theory, and cycle analysis techniques and applications can provide interesting articles for home computer buffs. The whole area of adaptive programs or programs that learn from experience hasn't been overdone so far as articles are concerned.

Novel or new language approaches, artificial intelligence, and robots provide even more article material. Ideas for computer simulation of physical phenomena, simpler computers, logical machines, and special purpose devices offers another field for article ideas.

By now you should be able to think of ideas for many other articles of this type. Don't forget to keep lists of ideas no matter how impractical they seem. Reading through these idea lists from time to time will trigger more new ideas. Let your subconscious mind work on these ideas while you're busy doing something else. Some of these ideas will provide you with new money-making opportunities that aren't even related to writing articles. The more effort devoted toward developing your creative abilities, the more successful you can become in all areas of life.

## Newsletters and Columns

Writing newsletters and columns differs from other writing activities in one important way: You are obligating yourself to produce a continuing stream of written material. The pressure imposed by predetermined deadlines may not appeal to everyone. It will also limit the amount of time you can devote to other money-making opportunities.

Most microcomputer magazines and several electronic publications run regular monthly columns on some aspect of microcomputers. If you can think of an area that might have wide interest and isn't being covered, you might have the basis for a new column. Of course, you must have some knowledge and ability in the area. In the future, home computer ownership should continue to grow rapidly, which might result in an opportunity for you to write a weekly home computer column in your local newspaper.

Publishing a newsletter also provides a spare-time income opportunity. Your newsletter should be based on a specific microcomputer or a specialized application area. Application areas might include health, education, gambling, investing, games, music, art, or any other activity that might provide enough subscribers to make a newsletter profitable. Advertising can also add to your profit if you can deliver enough potential customers. You should write letters to possible advertisers offering them attractive rates and pointing out the advantages of advertising in your newsletter. You can minimize your writing effort by publishing reader letters and comments. You can also pay nominal fees for articles or items of interest. You should advertise your newsletter in appropriate magazines to obtain subscribers. You can also sell programs or other products of your own through the newsletter for added income. Having several people involved in producing a newsletter is often a good idea. This allows for vacations, illness, or other time off without alienating subscribers.

It wouldn't be fair to conclude this section without mentioning what may be the best area for a newsletter. This type of newsletter is based on money-making opportunities in the microcomputer field. You will have lots of potential subscribers and advertisers. There will be no shortage of material. Case histories, new products, new opportunities, and tips from readers can all be covered. Sooner or later this type of newsletter will make someone rich. Will it be you?

### Construction Articles

Writing electronic construction articles is an excellent spare-time activity for advanced hardware hackers. The reason that it's a good opportunity involves the limited competition; high levels of skill are usually required. If you don't have the skill required to design new electronic devices, you may be able to find someone to design them for you. Maybe there's room for a hardware hacker's agent who will prepare and submit articles based on novel circuits or hardware designs. Try a small ad in one of the electronic magazines to see if there is any interest in this type of service.

Electronic construction articles have another interesting aspect. Small companies producing electronic construction kits are always looking for new products. If they like your construction project, they may be willing to offer it in kit form. You can be paid for the article and also collect a royalty on kit sales. The article even acts as an advertisement for the kit. If you have a new product in the form of an electronic construction kit, offer an article on it to magazines before you offer the kit for sale. You can advertise the kit in the article, but magazines generally won't buy an article describing a kit product that is already on the market.

Electronic magazines are looking for new, interesting construction projects for readers with a wide variety of interests and skills. The interests of these magazines aren't limited to microcomputers but include a wide range of gadgets and test instruments. Not all microcomputer magazines are interested in detailed construction projects. The ones that are usually want microcomputer modifications, attachments, or interfaces. Look through the magazines to get an idea of the types of construction articles that sell.

You must be sure that the project you describe in an article works. You must actually build it and test it to make sure. Most magazines want photographs of the completed project, a printed circuit board layout, a detailed parts list, and complete circuit drawings. You must provide the cost of the project and a source for any unusual or hard-to obtain parts. You should explain the theory of operation as well as construction details. Most magazines want a working model of your project before publishing your article. If this sounds like a lot of work, it is.

How do you get ideas for new electronic gadgets that would make good construction projects? These days it's easier than ever. New, low-cost integrated circuit chips are constantly appearing that can provide the basis for relatively easy construction projects. New electronic game, sound synthesis, memory, display, and even speech synthesis chips open up new construction project opportunities. Almost any special purpose gadget you might think of can now be constructed by combining a few integrated circuit chips on a small printed circuit board. These new chips can also be used with microcomputers. Several articles have described adding complex calculator chips to inexpensive microcomputers for improved computational ability. You can also easily attach to microcomputers chips for sound or speech synthesis, analog input-output, or motor control.

Less expensive microcomputer trainers, cheap stored program controllers, and security devices are candidates for construction articles. Inexpensive, special purpose computers can now be designed for almost any application and make ideal construction projects. The availability of nonvolatile memories that can be cheaply reprogrammed for specific applications make these special purpose microcomputer projects possible. Not too much has been written about the attachment of inexpensive special purpose microcomputers to larger general purpose microcomputers. Some interesting possibilities exist in this area.

Test instruments that appeal to hardware hackers provide opportunities for construction articles. You can turn inexpensive microcomputers into a variety of digital measuring instruments by adding photocells, temperature sensors, pressure switches, and analog input converters. With appropriate software you can measure or control motor speed, temperature, moisture level, or chemical reactions with a microcomputer. Biofeedback and biological monitoring devices are wide-open areas for new designs. Inexpensive aids for the handicapped are a real need that could be partially satisfied by construction articles. Educational devices and gadgets used with telephones lend themselves to construction articles.

Another interesting type of construction article would involve mechanical rather than electronic projects. Imaginative ways to package single card microcomputers, building computers into furniture, or wiring a house for microcomputer control could be covered. Mechanical attachments for microcomputers and various types of microcomputer-controlled robots are article candidates. New, inexpensive input devices such as simple punched card readers or light guns could be described. New battery-driven output devices or displays are possible. The area of inexpensive electromechanical gadgets for use with microcomputers is a fertile field for home inventors.

# 6

# Creating and Selling Programs

## Background

Many home computer hobbyists have writing and selling programs in mind when they buy a microcomputer. This can be an excellent spare-time money-making activity if you know what you're doing and approach it in a professional manner. The rapidly growing number of home computer owners will provide a continuing need for new software. The business market may provide fewer opportunities for part-time beginners. The reasons were discussed previously.

You will need your own computer, some programming ability, and good program ideas to succeed. This book can help you choose a microcomputer, tell you where to sell programs, and get you started in the idea department. You will have to develop the required programming ability on your own. Don't lose sight of the fact that you will face a lot of competition. As in any other field, your creativity coupled with a professional approach can give you an edge over the competition.

If you plan to license your programs to a specific microcomputer company, your choice of a computer is simplified. You will need the computer made by the company you want to sell programs to. If you want to license programs to a variety of possible software publishers, your computer choice is also relatively easy. Most major software publishers will be aiming their products at owners of the most popular microcomputers. This makes sense. The more people who own a specific computer, the larger the market for programs designed to run on it. In this case it pays to follow the crowd and buy the most popular home computer. If you plan to sell programs directly to customers, you might choose to specialize in a computer with a small dedicated following in order to minimize your competition.

After choosing your specific computer, you must decide on how much to spend for options. My opinion is that you should try to use the minimum system as much as possible if you plan to develop and license programs for the home market. The reason is obvious. The largest number of home users will own the least expensive version of the computer. There are plenty of new programs that can be written for minimum systems. Most major software publishers will accept programs in cassette form so that you don't even need a printer. If you are going to sell your own programs to specialized markets, then you might consider adding appropriate input-output options, including a printer. If you insist on writing programs for small businesses, you will usually need at least 16,000 bytes of memory and a floppy disc data storage unit. A high quality printer will also be needed for certain business applications, but not all.

After carefully choosing hardware based on your potential market, you have to choose your programming language. Most currently popular microcomputers have a built-in version of BASIC. You can use BASIC for your programs or write them in machine language. Sometimes machine language might be a better choice. For the Radio Shack TRS-80 minimum system, machine language programs permit faster loading of the data file, better game animation, interactive keyboard operation, and it overcomes a variety of limitations imposed by the built-in version of BASIC. Machine language programming can often provide better use of a small memory than BASIC does. The ability to program at the machine langauge level can be used to give you an edge over less skilled competition. You can always begin with BASIC programs and develop your machine language abilities at a later date if required.

When writing programs to submit to software publishers, remember that your submissions are being compared with large numbers of programs submitted by other programmers. Many of these other programmers will be more skilled than you. If you want to sell your programs to software publishers, you should do everything within your power to present yourself and your programs in the best possible manner. Start by maintaining a list of possible program ideas. This book will help you get started. Magazines and your imagination will help you get more new ideas. Try to add at least one new idea to your list every day. When you are ready to develop a new program, get out your list of ideas. Eliminate those that have been done already. Eliminate the ones that obviously exceed your existing hardware capability or current programming skill. Eliminate the ideas that are still too vague to be implemented. List the remaining ideas in order of probable user appeal. The ones that would appeal to the largest group of users should be at the top of the list.

Now spend some time deciding what you could say about each program. What user needs or desires does it satisfy? What can you tell users it will do for them? In other words, write a hard-sell advertisement for each potential program. You can limit this effort to the top five to ten ideas on your list.

Now you are ready to decide which idea to develop into a detailed program. Compare your ads for each potential program. Which ones make you want to buy the program? Pick the ad that has the most appeal. This is the program you should develop. Now try to improve your advertisement for this program. What else would you like to say about it? Incorporate these added appeals into the specifications for your program. You have now performed the most important part of writing a saleable program. You have selected the best ideas from the ones currently available to you. You have identified your market and its needs. You have written a hard-hitting advertisement for your program. You have approached program writing in a professional manner that gives you an edge over 90 per cent of your competition before you even begin any detailed programming.

Your next step will involve writing clear, detailed user instructions. Prepare a flow chart for your program. Give some extra thought to impressive graphics and humor, if appropriate. You can then write and debug your program. If you think you're through at this point, you're wrong. Test your program on family and friends. Observe their reactions. Incorporate any improvements that would make it better, more impressive, easier to use, and so on. Now sit down and rewrite your user instructions in final form. Write an introduction to your program aimed at users. This should provide a clear explanation of what the program does and how it does it. If there are user options or useful modifications possible, explain them clearly and in detail. Provide the user with exact memory requirements and loading instructions. Provide some simple tests the user can perform to verify that the program runs properly. Type this information in a pleasing format on a typewriter with a carbon film ribbon. Cheer up, you're almost finished.

Maybe you're wondering why so much effort is involved. You are being taught how to be a successful freelance product designer, not just a programmer. Most of your competition will be only programmers. Very few of them will be professional product designers. In this case, you will profit from being in the minority.

Your last step is a submission letter to your first choice software publisher. Never submit a program to more than one publisher at a time. The submission letter should be no longer than one page. It should be typed with a carbon ribbon on your personal or business letterhead. The letter should state that you're submitting the enclosed program cassette for possible publication on a royalty basis. Don't forget to label the cassette. Include your name as author. Don't ask for any specific payment terms at this time. The publisher will let you know the standard terms if there is any interest in your program. You will then be free to accept or reject the offer. Don't argue with a publisher who rejects your program. Offer it to another publisher. Your submission letter should include the hard-hitting advertisement you prepared initially. If this doesn't sell the program, nothing will. You should retain photo copies of all material sent to publishers, including letters. Request a return receipt from the post office when you send program material. If you don't hear from a publisher within six weeks, a gentle reminder that you're waiting to hear is in order.

If you object to the amount of effort detailed in the preceding paragraphs, you can take the same approach as many others. Sit down some evening after work or school. Turn on your computer. Bang out a quick and dirty version of the first program idea that pops into your head. Run it once to make sure there aren't any really obvious bugs. Grab a pencil and a crumpled sheet of yellow, lined paper. Write a note by hand to the effect that you'll license the enclosed program for a $2,000 advance. Make sure you have some misspelled and crossed out words. This shows publishers that you're a busy programming genius and they're lucky you wasted valuable time to submit anything to them. Send off your program and sit back and wait for your $2,000 check to appear in the mailbox. After six months of waiting, you can tell everyone that it's impossible to make money writing freelance programs because publishers don't recognize good stuff when they see it.

If you don't think this alternate approach will satisfy your desire for spare-time income, there is still one professional short cut you can take. Before you proceed with detailed programming, rewrite your advertisement in the form of a letter to a publisher asking if there's any interest in the program idea. If you get a positive reply, the same amount of work is required. Now, however, you're pretty sure of a sale. For negative replies you can try other publishers and other ideas before actually writing a program. The danger in this approach lies in your possible inability to follow through. You may run into unforeseen programming difficulties that require major concept revisions. If you can't provide what you promised initially, you can lose credibility with a publisher as well as losing the sale. This could hurt your chances for future sales to the same publisher.

### Where to Sell Programs

You can license or sell programs to software publishers, or you can produce and sell them yourself. The best approach will depend on the nature of the program and your own inclinations. This section discusses both approaches to provide a basis for your decision.

If your program has wide potential appeal and is designed to run on one or more of the most popular standard microcomputer systems, then selling it to an existing software publisher is probably your best choice. There are two ways to sell your program to a publisher. You can sell it outright for cash. Because there is no way of exactly predicting how well your program will sell, the publisher will decide on a probable value based on previous experience with similar types of programs. If you license your program to a publisher, you will receive a royalty on each copy of your program that the publisher sells. This royalty will generally be a fixed percentage of the price that the publisher receives. In either case, you receive money whether or not the publisher profits from your program. You may or may not receive a cash advance against future royalties when you license a program instead of selling it outright.

One program publisher is currently offering a 20 per cent royalty based on wholesale price. This would be about $1 per copy sold. This publisher sells programs in audio cassette form. If a cassette contains four small programs, only one of which is yours, then you would receive 25¢ per cassette sold. If this publisher were to sell 20,000 cassettes containing only your program, you would receive $20,000 in royalties. If 500 copies of your program were sold, you would receive $500. If your program was only one of four contained on the cassette, you could collect $125 to $5,000, depending on the number of cassettes sold.

You can now see how your choice of a computer can make a large difference in the amount of money you can make on a program. Suppose your program is written for a computer with 20,000 owners. Suppose you are lucky and your program has potential appeal for a quarter of these owners. Suppose you are lucky again and a quarter of these potential customers actually buy copies of your program. Starting with a base of 20,000 owners results in actual sales of 1,250 copies of your program. At a royalty of $1 per copy, you would make $1,250. Now suppose you had written your program for a home computer with 100,000 owners and that you had enjoyed the same amount of luck. You would make five times as much money, or $6,250, for the same amount of work.

You will receive more money from an outright sale of your program if sales fall well below the publisher's expectations. You will receive more money from a royalty arrangement if your program sells better than anticipated. I favor royalty arrangements because they don't limit the maximum you can make. At the same time, you probably don't stand to lose much relative to an outright sale. Any publisher who knows the business will offer you a cash price based on a conservative sales estimate. The chance that sales will fall much below this estimate is small.

Microcomputer companies, magazine or book publishers, and independents are the three types of program publishers. You should know a little about each so that you can decide which type to approach with your program.

Most microcomputer companies provide software for their products. Some of these programs are written by company employees, some are requested from freelance consultants, and some are written by outsiders like you. Microcomputer companies want programs that will help them sell computers and optional attachments. Slant your programs accordingly. You will obviously have to limit your submitted programs to those designed for products made by the specific company involved. If the company doesn't produce one of the more popular computers, you may not have a wide choice of alternative publishers if you strike out. A microcomputer company usually has a list of owners to whom it can send program advertisements. Don't choose a company that seems mainly interested in selling hardware and doesn't aggressively promote software.

Some microcomputer magazine and book publishers have also become program publishers. They represent a major opportunity for freelance program designers. *Kilobaud* and *Creative Computing* are two magazines that currently publish programs. They sell these programs in cassette form. Published programs are advertised for sale in the publisher's magazine and distributed through computer stores. Emphasis is on programs with wide appeal for owners of the most popular microcomputers. There must be a fairly large potential market for a program to justify the initial overhead cost of publishing it.

Independent software publishers are springing up in large numbers. It is obvious that new ones will continue to appear and that there will be an eventual shakeout. Which ones will survive is anybody's guess. You will have to be very selective in your choice of an independent software publisher. Read their ads in magazines and look in computer stores for their products. Try to pick those that have been around for a while and appear to be growing. To protect yourself, ask for a reasonable rather than a nominal cash advance. You may not get it, but at least you tried. The fact that you can't even get a token cash advance may give you a clue as to the financial status of the publisher.

Despite the risks, independent software publishers may be your best bet for certain types of programs. If your program is designed for a specialized computer with a relatively small number of owners, you might consider a small independent publisher. If your program has been rejected by major publishers, a small independent publisher may still be interested in it. Sometimes newsletters also publish programs to sell to their subscribers.

Instead of selling programs to publishers, you can become a software publisher yourself. You can have programs for popular computers duplicated on cassettes for less than $2 per cassette. One company currently performing this service is the Microsette Co., 777 Palomar Ave., Sunnyvale CA 94086. This takes care of your production problem. To the cassette cost you will have to add the costs of your time, advertising, and mailing. You can sell your own programs or buy programs from others to sell.

You can try to sell these programs through computer stores or by means of ads in computer magazines and newsletters. Advertising in hobby club publications is probably not a good idea because each club may buy only one copy of a program for its members. The biggest mistake you can make is underestimating the cost of your advertising. Be sure to write to magazines for their advertising rate schedules before you start. You will soon discover that advertising will be your single biggest cost.

You may want to concentrate on programs aimed at a specific application area such as music synthesis, gambling, or option trading. You may be able to find special interest areas that aren't big enough to attract the larger software publishers. At the same time there will be a big enough need for these specialized programs to make money for you.

In the following sections we try to get you started thinking about types of programs to write.

## Creative Recreation

There are two schools of thought regarding computers. A large group of computer people regard them as useful tools. A smaller group, to which I belong, views computers as super toys. Before Women's Lib there was a saying that you could tell men from boys by the price of their toys. Now you'd have to say that you could tell an adult from a kid by watching what their computers did. No matter how you view computers, there is no question that they can be fun. It is also a fact that the most popular home computer application so far has been playing games.

Hundreds of game programs have been designed for computers. Space War, Number Guessing, Tic Tac Toe, Chess, Checkers, Backgammon, Baseball, and Football have all been done. If you want to sell game programs, you can't simply duplicate old ones. You will have to come up with some new approaches. The word *game* tends to imply certain types of activities. Let's not restrict our thinking by using this term. *Creative recreation* is a better term. It includes all recreational computer applications.

For many home computer owners, the programming itself is a form of creative recreation. Can you think of ways to make programming 'easier and more fun for people? Can you provide special programming languages and techniques that give programming the same appeal as painting by number and other predesigned craft kits? How about easy animation languages to play with?

In the future people will want more exciting graphics in their games. Build your new game program around unique graphics if you want it to sell. Instead of simulating conventional sports or board games, try to come up with games that could be played only by using a computer. You might try games with invisible playing pieces or invisible obstacles. Dynamic games with objects moving around the TV screen that players have to dodge or catch make full use of the computer. The idea of two or more players preprogramming the movements of their playing pieces hasn't been exploited to any extent.

A number of computer games simulate real life or fantasy situations. Lunar Landing, Hammurabi, and Dungeons & Dragons are current examples. You should be able to dream up a wide variety of simulations on which to base recreational programs. Fantasy games and simulations are especially popular. The right approach can rapidly develop a cult following. Let your imagination run wild. Watch for popular fads that you might base games on.

Microcomputers make great toys. Not too much attention has been devoted to puzzles. Sliding block puzzles allow a variety of graphics, and they work well on a TV screen. How about TV puppets for young children? They can push buttons and make the puppets move or emit sounds. How about letting young children move three or four pieces of a super-simple jigsaw puzzle around the TV screen to form a geometric shape or picture? What other programs can you think of to turn a home computer into a toy for adults or for children to play with? A new idea in this area could be a big winner for you.

Not too much has been done in the way of adult party games, family games, or funny games for kids of all ages. How about a computer equivalent of the mousetrap game? Game packages that include boards and playing pieces used in conjunction with a computer program are a wide open field.

What kind of game programs can you design that will let people train and match their computers against each other? This is already being done in the area of computer chess. This type of activity has tremendous growth possibilities as home computers become more portable and the number of owners increases. Can you think of a programming game?

This could require a special language. Players might take turns adding instructions to a program. The first player to make the program perform a desired function wins.

There is a current trend toward minimizing the recreational aspects of home computers. Almost everyone in the computer business is sure that there must be a lot more important uses for home computers. I believe that recreation is an important home computer application and will remain so. You can make money from recreational home computer programs and have a lot of fun along the way.

## Educational Programs

Next to recreation, educational programs will be the biggest area for new home computer programs. As home computers gradually penetrate the educational system, there will be a slowly growing institutional market for educational programs as well as a large home market. There is a lot of confusion about the educational uses of computers. Most people think of educational applications in terms of showing questions or arithmetic problems on the TV screen and telling the user whether an answer was right or wrong. I take a broader view of the relation of computers to education.

Building a computer from a kit is educational. Programming a computer is the best sort of educational process. You learn about an area by breaking it down into small pieces and teaching it to a literal-minded machine. Making education fun results in a game. There is an educational aspect to all games. If you simulate something with a computer and let people experiment with this model, you have education by trial and error. This is an excellent way to learn, and computers make it possible. There is adult education and special education. There is almost no limit to the educational uses of computers. Home computers can help to satisfy real needs, and you can earn money by designing new educational programs.

Computer quizzes of all types are possible. They can be in the form of family or party games with scoring based on the time taken to respond correctly. Reflex and memory training can provide the basis for programs. Scoring for children should include graphics. Proper answers can help sink a boat, move an animal up a tree, or move a car on a race track. Use your imagination to provide motivating graphics. These types of programs can also be used by teachers in schools.

Educational programs aimed at home use will be your biggest market. Programs to help children with reading and math should be popular with parents and help to satisfy their need to rationalize the purchase of a home computer. Microcomputer companies may be a good market for these types of programs because the programs help to sell computers. There is a smaller market for programs that satisfy specialized educational needs in homes and schools. You might consider providing independent study packages for use in high schools. Can you design programs to help children with learning disabilities? You should work with teachers in designing your educational programs whenever possible. This will make your programs more acceptable to publishers, parents, and schools.

Simulation programs can be quite educational. A simulation program involves using the computer to imitate some other device or system. You can then learn by trial-and-error experiments with the simulated device or system. Aircraft pilots are trained on simulators. This prevents mistakes from being terminal. Physical experimental simulations can be used to teach principles of particle motion, force, momentum, friction, mechanics, or optics. System simulation programs can be used to teach money management, negotiating techniques, stock market trading, or gambling. Simulation games (with or without a computer) have been widely used as educational aids in schools and companies. Educational simulation programs for use with inexpensive microcomputers is certainly an area that hasn't attracted the amount of attention it deserves. You can still get in on the ground floor of this exciting area.

Computers are ideal for teaching problem-solving techniques. They are also perfect for teaching about computers. You can design programs for home computers that teach how to use and program the computer. You can simulate extremely simple tutorial computers to teach basic computer architecture and programming concepts. Learning about computers should become increasingly important because computers will increasingly influence everyone's life in one way or another. The microcomputer industry itself also provides an increasing number of new job opportunities, which is an added incentive for people to learn about computers.

As a Radio Shack ad states: "Tomorrow is an electronic world, based on computers—and it's already here. In it your child can be a number in a machine. A robot. Because he or she does not understand either the number or the machine. Or your child can be pleasurably elevated into this brave new world with a gift that has only become affordable in recent months." The thought expressed in this advertisement applies to most adults as well as to children. Lower cost home computers and appropriate programs can help more and more people learn about computers. You can make valuable contributions in the software area and earn extra money at the same time.

Computers can also be used to teach Morse code, touch typing, music, and a variety of other skills. Computer programs are easily adjusted to suit individual students and their ability levels. Using microcomputers in education is such a broad area that an entire book devoted to the subject would still only scratch the surface. You should have no trouble thinking up good ideas for programs in this area. It is destined to become a major growth area as new, lower cost microcomputers appear. New input-output techniques and devices will also permit an ever-wider range of educational programs to be designed.

## Home Management

Checkbook balancing, income tax preparation, recipe calculations, and budgeting are usually thought of as home management applications of computers. These activities represent only the visible tip of an iceberg. Home management and planning uses of microcomputers have a big future. In this chapter, home management and planning means those microcomputer applications involving the personal needs of home computer owners. These needs can be related to financial matters such as money management, beating inflation, saving money, investing, speculating, gambling, or increasing income. Another set of applications involves health needs related to diets, exercise, personal cycles, habits, illness prevention, rehabilitation, or overcoming handicaps. A third set of applications involves the quality of life needs or desires related to personal relations, mental outlook, security, comfort, career, job advancement, family planning, self-knowledge, self-improvement, consumer aids, and the planning of one's life style.

By now you should be starting to understand that this area involves more than simple checkbook balancing or recipe file programs. There is also a special problem for you in this area of home computer application. Most owners of home computers know that games can be fun or realize that educational programs can be useful. They don't, however, immediately realize what benefits they can obtain from many of the home management and planning programs that could be designed. If you are going to work in this area, plan to spend as much or more time on customer education as you will on program design. For example, with rational people there are techniques for developing personal profile graphs on a mathematical basis. One such possibility is a personal risk–reward preference curve that could be used to advantage in situations involving investment or speculation. The home computer can easily be used in developing and applying such curves. How many home computer owners do you think would immediately recognize the value of such an approach? Do you? Explaining the value of such new approaches to personal decision making could easily require as much effort as designing appropriate programs. This extra effort in explaining the benefits of your program will provide the difference between failure and success in this area.

Spend time in libraries and bookstores. Look through self-help, financial planning, investment, and gambling books for material you could use as a basis for new computer programs. Read through *this* book. Can you find ideas for programs that would help home computer owners make extra money with their computers? Could you design programs to help buy insurance, cars, homes, or real estate? Programs to keep records relating to hobbies or collections have been published. Can you think of other home inventory programs? How about computer diagnosis of typical houseplant, tropical fish, or pet problems?

Meal planning is often complicated in many families because of a variety of dietary restrictions for individual family members. How could a home computer help? A home computer could make it easier to hold a conversation with a deaf person. Programs can be used to specify and adjust various exercise routines. Inputs to such programs could include weight, blood pressure, and pulse rates before and after each exercise session. Home computers can also provide medication reminders and maintain records during an illness.

Biorhythm calculations are extremely popular even though they may not be too reliable. It is much more likely that people have unique cycles not related to standard numbers. The home computer can help people discover these cycles. Programs can permit keeping personal records relative to times and dates of low or high efficiency and can project these observed cycles into the future to help in work planning. Female cycles can also be extrapolated based on previous history.

Gambling is a way of life for many people. Sports handicapping is a natural application of the home computer. Your home computer could even pick lottery numbers for you. Stock and option trading systems provide the basis for all sorts of home computer programs and should prove to be increasingly popular with owners. Although a number of household budget programs already exist, there is plenty of room for improvement. Budget records can be used in programs that project the future financial status of a family based on a variety of assumptions. These assumptions can include variations relative to inflation, taxes, income, and future expenses. In other words, the computer could actually simulate the household economic system. The owner could use this customized model as a powerful planning tool on which to base current decisions.

Only the surface of home management and planning applications has been scratched, both in this discussion and in the home computer market. New programs in this area will fill real needs although people may have to be convinced that they have these needs. This is an area with a lot of growth potential. Programs you develop in this area can benefit you in two ways. You can use them yourself as well as making a profit from selling them.

## Business Programs

Common business computer applications include handling payroll, accounting, managing inventory, sorting mailing lists, and other standard data-processing operations. Many consultants, computer stores, and software publishers are concentrating their efforts in these types of small business applications. A number of new books are available in this area along with many older ones. As mentioned previously, these are not the types of applications emphasized in this book.

If you insist on competing in the small business area, then you might want to consider the approach outlined here. Look for a specialized small business and learn everything you can about it. Then look for potential microcomputer applications in the business. Find a local business of the type you studied and work with the owner in implementing your application program. After using it for a while, if you both agree that the microcomputer fills a need, you can proceed. Modify your program to cope with anticipated variations between individual businesses of the same type. You can then try to find a publisher who would be interested in your program. Instead of finding a publisher for your program, you might try to sell it to users directly. To do this you could place ads in appropriate trade publications. You might also try the direct mail approach, which requires sending advertising material directly to potential customers. In this case, your potential customers would be owners of the type of business for which your program was designed. Direct mail might be the best approach because you will have to explain a lot about computers as well as your program. Don't forget to tell potential customers exactly how a computer can help them, how little it will cost, and how much money (if any) they can save using your approach. Business customers will generally pay much higher prices for programs than typical home computer owners will.

Some types of small businesses that might be worth looking at are sales representatives, wedding or party consultants, home remodelers, horse farms or stables, animal dealers, antique dealers, aptitude testing services, art galleries, hi-fi system dealers, booking agents, bridge instructors, landscape services, caterers, nursery schools, coin dealers, restaurants, dog breeders, farmers, gift shops, equipment rental services, temporary help agencies, modeling agencies, health clubs, interior decorators, financial consultants, printers, astrologers, real estate investment consultants, and weight control services. This should be enough of a list to get you started. Now let's look at some types of computer applications that might be helpful to a few of these businesses. Remember that most business applications will require a more expensive computer system than generally required for home use. This added expense will most often involve a magnetic disc data storage unit or printer.

In the approach outlined here you're not looking for the conventional accounting type of application although it could be included with a complete software package for the selected business. Instead, you're trying to identify novel microcomputer applications that might give you an edge over what the competition is offering. One such application might be called "the computer expert" approach. This involves programming the computer so that it becomes a stand-in for the owner of the business. One common problem with many specialized small businesses is the owner. The success of the business is based mainly on the expertise or knowledge of the owner. This fact limits the potential size of the business and forces the owner to be actually present most of the time. The owner might be the only one who knows the current inventory or the availability of something not in stock. In many businesses, there are pricing or estimating rules of thumb that the owner has become expert in using.

Service businesses that involve scheduling available resources require a central scheduling control point—which is often the owner. The owner may also have variable pricing, priority, or payment rules for different customers or situations. Limiting the number of people who know these flexible rules is often the best policy for the owner.

Most of a business owner's specialized knowledge and rules for operating the business can be designed into a computer program. The information can be concealed in the program so that the owner need not worry about it's being revealed. Clerks or part-time help can then interrogate the computer instead of the owner in all but exceptional situations. This gives the owner much more personal freedom. It guarantees proper operation of the business in the owner's absence. This approach also minimizes the training problem associated with new, part-time, or temporary employees. Many small business owners are probably unaware of this type of valuable service that a small computer could perform for them.

Another small business computer application involves scheduling and planning. Wedding or party consultants are confronted with this type of problem continuously. A wide variety of options must be considered and combined into a complete event that meets a customer's price and time constraints. Then all the details must be scheduled and expedited to ensure a successful conclusion. A small computer with appropriate software should be extremely useful in this type of activity.

A hi-fi dealer is faced with the problem of assembling a variety of in-stock, compatible components into a complete system for customers. A computer program can easily perform this task. The computer has infinite patience with customers who want to examine all possible component and price combinations. The novelty value of computerized, custom design of audio systems could give the hi-fi dealer an advantage over the competition. It might also generate free publicity.

Some large chain stores have started to provide computers that allow customers to see if an item they want is in stock. Why not design software that lets smaller stores offer this service? A customer might also be able to ask the computer for gift ideas for a five-year-old girl or a seventy-three-year-old grandfather. Again, this would give the store an advantage over the competition. The store might even get free advertising in a local newspaper for the novel use of a small computer. The value of this free publicity could pay for the computer.

Visit small businesses and try to find unusual ways they could use inexpensive microcomputers. While most of your competition is fighting over the standard business applications, you can be designing specialized small business programs that make money for you.

## Novelty Programs

Novelty programs aim at unusual uses of home computers. Few programs of this type have been developed so far. Let your imagination run wild and see how many far-out ideas you can come up with. Maybe you'll discover the home computer equivalent of pet rocks and become an overnight millionaire!

Programs to calculate biorhythm cycles fall into the category of novelty programs and have proved popular. You might consider designing new fortune telling, numerology, or astrology programs for people to use. Imaginative programs relating to ESP or any of the so-called occult sciences might sell. These areas are extremely popular today, and combining them with computers could provide added appeal. You might provide programs aimed at helping people test or improve their ESP abilities. Along with programs in these areas, prepare printed material that provides background and application information. For example, if you were trying to sell a biorhythm program, you would include examples of how these cycles related to major events in the lives of famous people. You would then point out how biorhythms might relate to the future performance of football teams or boxers. The material accompanying the program would then show how users could perform biorhythm research into past events in their own lives. Children could even use the biorhythm program for extra-credit study projects in school by correlating historical events with the biorhythm charts of the people involved in the events.

Everyone who owns a home computer needs flashy demonstration programs to show off their hardware to friends. Many game programs aren't very impressive unless you know something about computers. Fancy graphics and other novelty programs can really impress most people more than games. Unusual and exciting demonstration programs could be best-sellers. Speaking of demonstration programs, animated TV screen graphics can make superb holiday and party decorations or conversation pieces when friends drop by. Birthdays, Halloween, and Christmas lend themselves to such graphics. Preparing the graphics requires imagination and work. Most home computer owners would probably be glad to buy such a program if good ones were available.

Humorous novelty programs seem to be a neglected area. Could it be because programmers don't have a sense of humor? There could be a good market for such programs if you can create them. An ego-building program would provide compliments on demand. A scheduling program for procrastinators has been urgently needed for some time. No one seems to have gotten around to writing one yet. Many times it's hard to justify delays without the aid of a computer. How about funny aptitude tests or lie detectors? A computer hypnotist or "shrink" might have some appeal if done properly. Computerized "mad libs" should be popular with the party set.

Owners of home computers might be interested in buying programs that let them experiment with patterns. Programs that make it easy to create TV pictures or animation should be popular. Users can become instant electronic artists. Programs can even provide soothing, ever-changing TV displays that have the same appeal as the specialized equipment of light shows. In some computers it's even possible to synchronize the TV display to hi-fi music with appropriate software.

Another unusual type of program involves simulation. It is sometimes possible to simulate one computer on another. Programs to do this are generally written in machine language. If you write a program that lets one computer simulate another, then you can run programs designed for the computer being simulated without actually owning the simulated computer. There could be a market for programs that permit simulating an older computer on a newer more popular one. This would make software available for the older computer usable on the newer machine. Simulation can be tricky, and you had better stay away from it if you're a beginner.

There has been no attempt to cover all possible unusual or humorous home computer software ideas. It could be a rewarding area if you have a warped, inventive mind! If you are a more conventional type of thinker, then you will find plenty of new program possibilities in the areas of games, education, and specialized applications for small business.

## New Opportunities

Prices of home computers will continue to drop. Lower microcomputer prices will greatly improve your chances to make money by writing programs. Lower prices mean many more home computer owners, which in turn lets you make more money per program. For example, if there are now 50,000 owners of a specific computer, you might sell a program to 5 per cent of these owners for a profit of $2,500. This assumes a $1 profit or royalty for each copy of your program that is sold. Now suppose that microcomputer prices drop to the point at which there are 500,000 owners of a specific home computer. Selling your program to 5 per cent of this market would give you a total profit of $25,000 for the same amount of effort. Freelance program design should become much more financially interesting in the future.

As new microcomputers and input-output devices appear, your opportunities to design and sell new programs will improve. As pointed out earlier, the uses of a computer are limited by its input-output capabilities as well as available software. As new input-output capabilities are made available to owners of home computers, the types of programs you can design will increase. Some new capabilities to watch for include inexpensive music, sound effects, and voice output. Computer telephone attachment capability will decrease in price. New low-cost biofeedback capabilities will be added. It's not too early to plan ahead. You can be thinking of programs to exploit new input-output capabilities when they become widely available. This will give you a head start in writing saleable new programs as soon as the market needs them.

Another factor that can increase your opportunities for new program profits will be the increasing sophistication of home computer owners. Right now, most owners don't appreciate the value of many potential home computer applications. They will be hung up on games and educational applications for a while. Eventually they will become ready for home or personal management and planning applications. You can be ready for the shift in application emphasis when it occurs. Think of the current phase of the microcomputer industry as your opportunity to develop the skills that can make really big money for you in the future.

# 7

## Services for Sale

### Consulting

Chapters 5 and 6 described a number of opportunities in the areas of writing for money and selling programs This chapter covers various microcomputer services you could provide in your spare time. Consulting is the first type of service discussed.

Consulting involves getting paid for your knowledge and advice. Of course, you'll have to have some knowledge that people will be willing to pay for. A consultant is generally thought of as an outside expert who is paid for advice or guidance in a specialized area. Microcomputers are considered to be a specialized area by most people. To make money, you will have to find people who are willing to pay for your advice. There are a lot of microcomputer consultants around so you will have competition. Your best chances to make money will be in areas that are ignored by most consultants. You can specialize in these areas. Because consulting will be a spare-time activity, you should look for opportunities that don't involve expensive, time-consuming travel.

Many microcomputer consulting opportunities involve small business applications. Normally, small business owners have little or no computer knowledge and require guidance in choosing hardware and developing appropriate software. They often depend on consultants for this guidance. Most computer stores and independent consultants are concentrating their efforts on small business owners. They guide owners toward the standard small business computer applications comprising accounting and other conventional data-processing operations. Go back and re-read the section on business programs in Chapter 6. The approach taken there involved specializing in novel small business applications of microcomputers instead of the standard ones. You could also aim your consulting activities toward these unconventional microcomputer applications. You could specialize in developing the types of programs described in Chapter 6. Your consulting activity would then involve showing appropriate small business owners how your approach could help them, recommending appropriate hardware and tailoring the software to individual businesses. You could sell the programs, charge a fee for your service, and try to obtain a sales commission on hardware. Your best way to obtain customers involves contacting local businesses and arranging demonstrations of your approach for them.

As an independent consultant, you can help people decide whether or not they could use a small computer effectively. You could help them get started at minimum expense. You would have an advantage over computer stores or computer sales representatives. The customer knows that selling hardware would not be your primary goal. Your advice also would not be biased toward specific types of hardware that you happen to have in stock or on which you receive the largest mark up. Most small business owners will be quick to recognize these factors. You could function as a preliminary consultant who refers the small business owner to a computer store after making a rough initial analysis of his needs and providing general guidelines for him to follow. You would really be providing a microcomputer tutoring service that prepares the small business owner to talk to computer salesmen without being deceived by sales talk. You might also consider offering your services to a local computer store as a part-time consultant for them. You could be most effective in locating and screening potential customers.

You could also specialize in another business-related activity. Microcomputers can be used effectively for advertising, promotion, and traffic building. You could become a consultant in these specialized areas. The section that deals with renting your computer discusses this area in more detail.

Your consulting opportunities aren't limited to owners of small businesses. Schools, museums, potential buyers of home computers, churches, and clubs could all use your guidance on purchasing microcomputers. Again, you would provide educational consulting as to possible applications, available hardware, and appropriate software.

One of your best opportunities might be to become a low-priced, mail-order consultant. You could fill a real need, and the area seems to have been overlooked so far. It is similar to selling information by mail. In this case the information is customized for individual customers. Let's look at one way this idea might be implemented.

There are thousands of subscribers to microcomputer magizines who don't own a computer yet. They are constantly reading about different computer types, prices, features, languages, and input-output devices. In many cases, they are getting more confused about what to buy and when. Here's where you come in. They see your advertisement offering free details on your consulting service, which can provide personalized guidance in computer selection and use. When you receive an inquiry, you send back a detailed description of your services and prices. Explain how the service can save them money and time. It will prevent them from making the costly mistake of buying the wrong hardware for their needs. They can receive additional help in using their hardware after purchase.

What services can you provide? You can first supply a standard questionnaire for the customer to fill out and send back to you. The form would include the customer's background, ability level, interests, goals for computer use, and financial constraints. You could then recommend an appropriate approach. This approach might involve a single card computer or a complete system. Advice would include the least expensive way for the customer to achieve his microcomputer goals. Additional services you could provide would include references to books and articles appropriate to the customer's specific needs. You could also provide sources of parts, specialized microcomputer attachments, or specific application programs. In other words, you would be a personal adviser for people interested in owning and using home computers. Much of your advice would involve helping customers organize their thinking, plan their approach, and avoid major pitfalls. I have talked to hundreds of owners of home computers who could have benefited greatly from such advice. You could even use your computer to print out customized advice or information.

Mail-order consulting can also involve other areas. You could act as an advertising consultant for small companies and individuals selling products or services related to microcomputers. In Chapter 5 the pencil for hire section suggested another form of consulting service involving the design of instruction manuals.

Maybe you collect books and magazines on home computers. If you do, and if you also read everything you see on the subject, you may be an expert on where to find specific information. You can charge a fee for your knowledge. Run a small ad in microcomputer magazines offering to provide references to specific types of information desired by readers. You might even provide copies of hard-to-locate or out-of-print articles. Clipping services get paid to read publications and provide copies of items that mention specific products or authors. Authors or companies pay a nominal fee for each item sent to them. Maybe you could make a few extra dollars by providing this type of service for the microcomputer industry.

There are two roads to part-time consulting success. First, you can look for unusual microcomputer applications that you can specialize in on a local basis. The second approach involves mail-order consulting, in which you would provide customized variations of standard information or advice for modest fees. Be sure that you adopt a professional approach to either area.

## Hardware Services

To sell hardware services you must be a hardware hacker or own specialized equipment. The services are aimed at people who don't have hardware skills or who need temporary access to special equipment.

There are a variety of microcomputers and attachments that come in kit form. Assembling these kits properly can pose a problem for beginners. You can charge a nominal fee to assemble kits for these beginners. You can also specialize in computer repair. Servicing cassette recorders, TV displays, printers, and magnetic disc devices can become a money-making activity for you. Hardware modification represents another opportunity for you. Many computer owners would like to have standard TV sets modified to act as video monitors. Modifications for expanding memory, providing upper and lower case TV display, adding dual language capability, and making cassette recorders easier to use are possible with certain popular microcomputers. You can get paid to install these modifications for owners who don't have the required hardware skills. You can easily find modification instructions and kits by reading microcomputer magazines. You might consider offering part-time services of this type to your local computer store. You can also advertise these services in the publications of local hobby clubs.

The installation and maintenance of security systems controlled by microcomputers is another spare-time hardware service that can make extra money for you. Don't forget that many arcade games are based on microcomputers and require repair services. Special memory chips that can have programs permanently stored in them are becoming popular. A low-cost attachment for your computer would let you customize these memory chips for individuals without this capability.

Customized microcomputer design comprises a major money-making hardware service. It is often classified as a form of consulting. Many owners of home computers need a special attachment designed and installed for a specific application. This need can often be met by providing a slight modification of an existing product. You can profit by filling this type of need. You can also become a specialist in modifying standard microcomputers for use in high school science labs. Most high school teachers aren't aware of how easily inexpensive microcomputers can be used to monitor and control lab experiments. A low-cost, single card microcomputer with suitable modifications and software can often replace more expensive equipment. You might also consider specializing in modifying microcomputers for use by handicapped people or special education schools. This activity could fill a real need at the local level and can provide an extremely satisfying spare-time activity. Local museums may be interested in incorporating microcomputers into their displays. This would be an interesting opportunity for you to investigate.

Many inexpensive programmable video games could be programmed for specialized educational or advertising displays. Such applications would involve providing special plug-in program modules. Special Read Only Memory (ROM) chips permit you to produce such modules. Your major problem would be to learn the programming language used in these games and to develop software using this language. The companies providing these products probably aren't interested in exploiting custom, small-volume applications. Whether they would provide you with enough information to pursue these applications would have to be determined. Companies can be expected to make these games programmable by owners in the future. Even if customized video game applications aren't practical for you to pursue right now, keep it in mind for the future.

Many small local companies are becoming increasingly interested in possibilities for using microcomputer technology in their products. They may have very little microcomputer knowledge and no skill. You may be able to provide them with useful ideas and even detailed assistance on product design on a part-time basis. This type of activity could also lead to future full-time job opportunities for you.

Another novel hardware business opportunity should be mentioned. Video games together with a TV set can be built into furniture such as cocktail tables. Used video games can be turned into saleable custom-made products in this way. Custom furniture with built-in general purpose microcomputers is also a possibility.

Last but not least, you might consider becoming a local dealer in used microcomputers. This would tie in nicely with a small microcomputer repair shop. New microcomputers appear so fast that a large supply of obsolete products will be building up. At the same time, there will be many potential microcomputer owners who can't afford the price of a new computer. You may be able to buy older microcomputers, recondition them, and sell them to new owners at a reasonable profit. Don't forget that microcomputers include special purpose devices such as electronic toys and video games.

### Software Services

Chapter 6 described designing and selling programs. It told how to write a program and make money by selling multiple copies of it. In this section, we discuss writing one-of-a-kind programs for spare-time income. If you have any degree of programming skill, you should be able to sell it on a part-time basis. Custom programming services are often needed by most computer owners. Your major pitfall will involve getting in over your head. Here are some guidelines that will help you. Make sure you know exactly what's involved in any custom programming job you tackle. Work out a detailed written specification of the program with your customer before you begin. Avoid situations in which customers aren't exactly sure of what they want, have unrealistic goals for microcomputer application, or are constantly changing their minds. You'll always lose money in these situations, and your reputation will suffer from having an unhappy customer. Be selective. Choose well-defined, small programming jobs on a specific system that you are sure you can handle. Avoid large, complex programming jobs. Figure out realistically how long it should take you to write and debug the customer's program. Give your customer an estimate that is twice as long as you calculated. You can always reduce your fee if a job turns out to be easier than expected. Raising your fee halfway through a job makes customers unhappy and reduces your credibility. Jobs seldom turn out to be easier than expected.

You can offer custom programming services to individuals, companies, schools, and owners of small businesses. Computer stores may be able to use part-time programmers for their customers. Program publishers might be able to use part-time programming services. One publisher currently intends to use freelance programmers to review, test, and improve programs submitted for publication. Publishers may also pay to convert a program designed for one computer so that it will run on other popular systems.

Another software service opportunity is to be a specialist in a certain type of program. One example is programming languages. Suppose you write a new language interpreter that receives publicity in articles or books. Microcomputer companies might be willing to pay you to adapt it for use on their specific computers. In other words, you can become an expert in writing a specific type of program efficiently. This will usually involve some special algorithms or techniques you've developed. It will now pay companies who want this type of program written to come to you. Programmers have made money using this approach in the areas of BASIC, FORTH, chess software, and adventure games. What areas can you become an expert in?

There are opportunities in the area of software services that don't involve custom programming. Individuals writing software articles may need high-quality printouts of their programs. If you have a printer, you can provide this service for a nominal fee. Customers send you program cassettes, and you mail back as many printed copies of their program as needed. You might consider adding circuits to your computer that permit you to cope with a variety of popular recording formats for cassette tapes.

One possible hardware service described in the previous section was the design of custom microcomputers or interfaces. The design of custom software will also be required for use with this nonstandard hardware. There is a variety of opportunities for you to supply custom programming services to hardware designers. You could even offer to collaborate with hardware hackers who need software help in writing an article or book. Many home computer owners might need custom written subroutines to interface with specialized microcomputer attachements. Schools can be a market for a variety of custom programs designed for classroom and lab use.

Writing custom programs for owners of microcomputers can give you experience with a variety of different applications. This is one way of getting ideas for programs to sell. If one local owner needs a specific type of program written, then the chances are that a lot of other owners could use the same program. Sometimes you only have to make a few changes in a program designed for a specific user in order to make it useful to many other people.

## Renting Your Computer

Microcomputer rental appears to be an untapped source of ideas for spare-time income. You could rent microcomputers by the day or by the week for a variety of purposes. This activity is, by nature, a small local business. In many cases, you can buy used hardware for rental purposes, thus keeping your capital outlay low. After all, the computers will become secondhand after you rent them.

Many people have discovered that video games are popular at parties and ideal for entertaining ill children or shut-ins. You could investigate renting the more expensive video games to people for these purposes. Maybe local gift or party supply shops would cooperate in this venture. Hospital or institutional rentals represent another opportunity. Classified ads in local newspapers might provide you with customers. If video games with their limited capabilities are popular, then being able to rent a real computer complete with a library of party games should have even more appeal. As prices of general purpose microcomputers drop, so would your rental prices. A big selling feature would be the programs you can supply for party games and activities.

You should be able to rent microcomputers with appropriate programs for special educational needs that might include learning touch typing or Morse code. Temporary special drills or tutoring for young children could provide a reason to rent a computer. Many parents rent a piano to determine a child's interest before spending a large amount of money to buy one. Home computers could be rented for the same purpose, and the family adults could test their interest as well. You might arrange a commission for yourself on a subsequent sale of the computer. The software you develop or supply to the potential customer is your key to success. Try to determine family interests and supply appropriate software. You might try advertising this type of rental service on school bulletin boards. For home trial rentals you should prepare a brief, easy-to-use introduction to programming that uses a language such as BASIC. The introduction should be designed so that family members will actually be able to write and run some short, simple programs with a minimum of time and effort spent in learning. Most people never get hooked on programming because they never have the opportunity.

As the cost of word-processing systems comes down, another rental opportunity will be created for devices known as microcomputer controlled typewriters. These devices let you compose lines on a display screen, make corrections, and store the lines in memory. You can call up common phrases or words with single keystrokes. You can recall previously stored data at any time for correction. After completion, the stored data are automatically typed. These machines make typing much easier. You could rent them on a temporary basis to authors, students, or anyone faced with a large, short-term typing job.

There is another major computer rental area that you might want to specialize in—that is, advertising applications for microcomputers. Almost every store and shopping mall would be a potential customer. You would require some imagination along with suitable hardware and software. Inexpensive microcomputers with video displays could be used for attention-getting window and inside displays. Eye-catching animated graphics could be integrated with the desired advertising message. You might want to dress up the computer in an attractive wooden cabinet for advertising displays. You could use inexpensive, secondhand, single card computers and used TV sets in these custom-built programmable advertising displays. You could develop some standard display software in which it's easy to change the advertising message. You could rent these units, which are ideal for special sales, openings, and so on, to stores by the week or month. Shopping malls could use them to display special event calendars or data on individual stores. Displays of this type could be put together for several hundred dollars in hardware costs. You might be able to break even in as few as ten weeks of rental.

You can get even fancier with your rented advertising displays. You might add more storage capability and let shoppers have access to the computer by means of a rugged keyboard or several pushbuttons. Then you would have an interactive advertising display that could answer a limited set of customer questions. Humorous displays that ask the customer trick questions or supply funny answers to customers' questions could be real attention getters and traffic builders.

Simple games such as tic-tac-toe always seem to draw a crowd. Programs that display fortunes, biorhythms, or horoscopes are crowd pleasers. Short lists of gift suggestions could be provided. New books could be advertised. An inexpensive printer could be incorporated if desired. Various contests and promotional stunts could be designed around the computer. As microcomputer prices drop, the advertising applications of microcomputers should gain in popularity. Imaginative specialists in this area will be needed.

## Get Your Act Together

The preceding section discussed opportunities related to renting microcomputers. This section discusses teaming yourself up with a microcomputer and appropriate software. You would then be ready to go on the road with a new act that could make some extra money for you in your spare time. You probably won't be as popular as a rock group, but you should be able to get paid for a few one-night stands. Now let's see what kind of saleable acts you might be able to come up with. We'll keep in mind the fact that your acting, singing, or musical talents may be underwhelming. You should not let this fact discourage you from considering a part-time career in show business. If politicians can do it without any visible talents, so can you.

Your first show business activity might involve entertaining at children's parties. You'll need a funny hat, a funny costume for your computer, and some entertaining programs. If you're a professional programmer, you can dress normally. But seriously, folks, if amateur clowns and magicians can do it, why can't you and your crazy computer be a hit with the kids and their parents? You'll need to develop some party game programs and figure out some magic tricks involving the computer. You might even work out a comedy mindreading act in which you blindfold the computer. Give this area some thought. You may discover some well-hidden talents and a latent sense of humor that your friends never noticed. If you come up with a good enough act, you may even start being invited to adult parties. This can be your stepping stone to the really big time . . . trade shows, club meetings, and luncheons.

The previous section described advertising applications of microcomputers. You can also team up with your computer for shopping center promotions involving entertaining demonstrations. These types of promotions have involved card sorters and remote controlled robots dressed as people. You should be able to think of some attention-getting demonstrations involving microcomputers.

There are a number of part-time teaching opportunities. You might consider teaching evening adult education courses in microcomputers. You might be able to teach introductory hardware or programming courses for local computer stores. Various business groups or other clubs might be willing to pay for educational and entertaining microcomputer talks. There may be part-time teaching possibilities at local schools or colleges. You might offer tutoring in programming at your home or the student's home, similar to services offered by piano teachers. You could offer introductory computer classes for specific groups of owners of small businesses. Always remember that teaching is a branch of show business. The most popular and successful teachers are entertaining enough to motivate students and keep them awake.

To bring down the curtain on our discussion of show business, let's examine opportunities in microcomputer sales. If you don't believe selling is related to show business, you have never watched used car dealers do their act. Selling microcomputers can provide a spare-time money-making activity for you. A variety of approaches can be taken. For example, a computer store might be willing to pay you a commission if you find customers for them. A good way to find customers would be as a result of consulting, teaching, or demonstration activities. If you have developed an unusual application program that you are demonstrating and attempting to sell to a specific type of small business, you are in an ideal position to sell the required hardware as well. If you are providing consulting services for schools, you may be able to add to your income by commissions on hardware sales. Renting computers for home use can also lead naturally to subsequent sales.

You might also try your hand at some novel sales techniques for home computers. Right now, people who want home computers have to dig through microcomputer magazines to find out what's available and how they can use it. They must go to a computer store for a demonstration. The computer store may not spend much time with potential buyers of home computers because they are often mistaken for casual lookers. Computer stores also tend to be more interested in selling higher priced systems to owners of small businesses. Many clerks in computer stores really don't know very much about computers or applications. Currently, many of them aren't very effective salesmen. I have received a lot of bad advice and information from disinterested clerks in computer stores. This is true of any retail operation in any field. Only the most persistent or knowledgeable customers finally buy a home computer. There are hundreds of thousands of people who might buy a home computer if they kenw what it was and how they could use it. Computer stores evolved because there is so much education and demonstration involved in selling home computers. Unfortunately, the stores are aiming their best efforts at business customers, which leaves an unfilled marketing need in the area of computers. How can this need be met?

New buyers of home computers can be developed by a series of steps. By giving entertaining microcomputer talks and demonstrations at schools and clubs, you can generate interest in owning a microcomputer. To actually recruit new customers there is no substitute for going directly into homes. Fortunately, you don't have to go door to door with your sample case like the Fuller Brush or Avon person. Instead, you can arrange home computer parties. These types of parties are being used to sell all sorts of things; why not home computers, too? People love any excuse to get together. Through personal contacts or local newspaper ads, you locate people willing to host a home computer party. They in turn invite a bunch of friends who are compatible, interested in a free evening get-together, and possibly even mildly curious about home computers. You can guarantee the hosts a fun evening, a free book on home computers and a discount if they purchase a home computer through you. You now have your opportunity to convince a group of people that a home computer is something they really need and want. You should, of course, have a really entertaining and effective presentation planned to include fun, games, and educational applications. You should show how easy computers are to use and how inexpensive they are when compared with hi-fi systems, school tuitions, or vacation costs. You should have exciting material to hand out with your name, address, and phone number prominently displayed on it. Don't forget to demonstrate horoscopes and football handicapping. Explain your trial rental service for home computers.

Having read this book, you probably already know more about potential applications of home computers and how to sell them than 95 per cent of the people professionally involved in the microcomputer industry. Maybe you could convince your favorite computer store or computer company to sponsor your party plan approach to selling home computers.

# 8

# Use Your Imagination

## Arts, Crafts, and Novelties

If you have artistic talent, imagination, manual dexterity, and a sense of humor, the microcomputer industry provides you with some more new spare-time money-making opportunities. Some of these opportunities involve handmade products that would appeal to owners of home computers. You might try to sell these products in local computer stores, gift shops, or craft shows. You could also advertise your products in newsletters, club publications, or magazines. Typical products could include jewelry, stuffed pillows, novelty figures, or sculpture.

Computer-related jewelry might appeal to computer owners. Rings, pins, tie clips, or pendants could be made using real microcomputer chips, which would be reject chips purchased from the manufacturer. Custom jewelry can also incorporate the name of a specific home computer club or hobby club in its design. Novelty hardware bugs could be designed using resistors, nuts, bolts, and the like. Paperweights with specific microcomputer chips imbedded in them make interesting conversation pieces. Stuffed program bugs or seat cushions for giant brains might sell. Be sure to include a printed information card with novelty items of this type.

People interested in home computers might also like various types of electronic sculpture. Dual in-line integrated circuit packages could have faces painted on them and be made into novelty figures. You've probably seen similar items that use nails or painted stones. Your little sculptures made from integrated circuit packages could be labeled as chip off the old block, chip and putt, chips ahoy, or chocolate chip, for example. You probably get the idea. More sophisticated electronic sculpture could be made from Plexiglas, light emitting diodes (LEDs), integrated circuits, and speakers. This type of sculpture could be powered by a battery in the base and have flashing lights and weird sounds. The possibilities for artistic experimentation are endless. Some forms of electronic sculpture could be provided in kit form for people who like to build things.

Some of your artistic or novelty designs might even be sold to publishers or other companies interested in computer-related products. You might want to obtain copyright or patent protection for designs that could be sold to other people to manufacture.

Posters, computer art prints, greeting cards, and bumper stickers can be designed for computer freaks. Posters could depict magnified integrated circuits, which can be quite striking. Posters could also provide caricatures of hardware hackers or programmers doing their thing. Stationery and humorous business cards could be designed for computer buffs. Funny bumper stickers are always popular. Greeting cards for computer people might have the greeting or message contained in a short BASIC program, and they could also incorporate computer art. A gag computer operator's license could be provided.

Many personalized products for computer owners could make successful mail-order items if advertised in microcomputer magazines. Custom T-shirts for specific computers or clubs could be popular. Personalized name plates, stationery, cassette labels, and bookplates are a few more examples.

Other novelty products might include computer books for children that could be punched out and assembled. Joke novelties could include a write-only memory, a solid state graphic display device (pencil), and a checkbook balancing system for home computers. The latter would consist of a wire frame that would let you balance a real checkbook on top of your computer. Computer novelty items should increase in popularity as the number of owners grows and the public becomes more sophisticated. This area can provide you with a lot of fun. Any time you feel that dreaming up novelty ideas is foolish, just think about the money that somebody made from Pet Rocks. Someday your pet chip, square disc, floppy floppy, program bug, or invisible computer might make money for you. Remember that in these areas people aren't really paying for the product. They're buying the concept and the humor contained in the written instructions for use.

Don't overlook new electronic novelty items. New integrated circuits can produce inexpensive sounds, flash lights, and even talk. Remember how popular inexpensive laughing boxes were? In the future, electronic laughing boxes will be popular. These little boxes can provide insults or compliments on demand. They can count to ten or swear for you. Maybe the world is ready for an inexpensive flying saucer detector!

Returning to the area of handmade arts and crafts, some readers may have a general interest in this area. If you are interested in this area aside from any microcomputer tie-in, there is an interesting book on the subject called *How To Make Money With Your Crafts* by Leta W. Clark. It's published by William Morrow and Co., Inc., 105 Madison Ave., New

York, NY 10016. You may see it in bookstores, or you can order it from the publisher. It costs about $3 in paperback and is a good reference book for people who are interested in selling handmade items or art.

## Games, Gadgets, and Tools

Here are more types of products you can think about creating. Some of these creations might be patentable. The next chapter discusses inventing in more detail. Creating a popular new game, puzzle, toy, or gadget can make you a lot of money. For example, a game or toy that enjoys only average popularity can have sales of 500,000 units. If you make only ten cents on each sale, you would make $50,000. You should try to come up with computer-related games or toys that appeal to a wide market, not only to owners of home computers. I have had success with plastic games using marbles that are based on binary computer principles. Of course, there is nothing wrong with creating games, gadgets, and tools aimed at computer owners. The market is limited now, but you can make money with such items, and your market is sure to grow in the future.

Jigsaw puzzles are always popular. New ones depicting magnified integrated circuits, printed circuit boards, program flowcharts, or computer-generated art should appeal to a wide market. Can you create some new types of plastic puzzles? Look through stores to get an idea of the types of adult puzzles being sold. Inexpensive computer-related games or puzzles could make good advertising premiums for computer stores or companies.

There is a variety of game approaches you might think about. Educational games that provide an introduction to computers or programming could be a good area. Can you develop a game that teaches BASIC programming? Board or card games could be based on logic diagrams or program flowcharts. Many computer game programs might be converted into low-cost plastic or cardboard versions. The best-selling *Mastermind* game incorporates the idea of guessing the hidden number used in early computer programs. Video tennis games inspired an inexpensive mechanical version, which became extremely popular. *Lunar Landing* and *Life* are two computer games that might be used as the basis for inexpensive consumer games. Can you think of others?

Don't forget that your computer can also help you in designing games. You can simulate various games on your computer to determine play value. The computer can actually run through thousands of simulated games using different rules. You can use computer runs to fine-tune game rules or eliminate possible player biases. The computer can help you find bugs in game rules that might permit a player unfairly to prevent other players from winning by endlessly repeating a short sequence of moves.

New electronic games based on microcomputer technology are currently selling extremely well. Maybe you can think of new winners in this area. Look at the ones currently being sold to get an idea of the price and levels of technology involved. Maybe you can come up with an electronic Ouija board or an electronic *Name That Tune* game. You will probably have a better chance in this area if you're a hardware hacker.

Gadgets and tools related to home computers represent another area of growth to investigate. Look at all the kitchen, car, and photographic gadgets being sold. There must be a variety of possible new gadgets that would relate to home computers. Dreaming them up could be a way for you to make lots of money. How about a Polaroid camera stand for photographing TV screen displays? One company is selling a small box to provide more convenient cassette connection to the TRS–80 computer. A box to match this computer's video output to standard video monitors could easily be designed. One way to invent new gadgets is to think in terms of possible needs that hardware hackers or programmers might have. This could give you ideas for inexpensive gadgets or tools to satisfy these needs.

Hardware hackers comprise a market for gadgets or tools that make it easier for them to build and test electronic circuits. Solder removal braid, integrated circuit test clips, logic probes, and solderless breadboarding systems are specific types of gadgets and tools being sold to satisfy the needs of hardware hackers. You don't have to be a hardware hacker to think up these aids. You do have to observe hardware hackers and be able to perceive unsatisfied needs. Hardware hackers also want to learn about new integrated circuit chips. Inexpensive kits that permit them to experiment easily with new chips could help to satisfy this desire.

Programmers need things to make it faster and easier to write and debug programs. Special coding forms, flowcharting systems, or instruction reference cards are aids that help to satisfy this need. Could you provide a deck of cards that would permit rapid construction of certain types of programs? Each card might contain a subroutine for a common function. Programs could be designed by arranging the cards on a table top. Structured programming techniques lend themselves to this form of modular program construction. Different sets of cards could be provided for different classes of programs. You could include specific program examples and suggestions for new programs. This would be an ideal approach for beginners or inventors of game programs.

Several years ago there was an inexpensive educational computer simulator on the market called CARDIAC. This device illustrated the principles of stored program computer operation. It was probably ahead of its time. With the much wider interest in computers now, and the availability of microcomputer magazines to advertise in, educational gadgets of this type should do much better.

Coming up with imaginative new games, gadgets, and tools that are related to microcomputers is an excellent spare-time money-making activity. Most people involved with home computers tend to ignore this area. They understand that writing articles, books, and programs might be profitable, but they fail to understand that games, gadgets, and tools can be even bigger money makers for them. Make sure you don't get so involved with the technical details of computers that you forget about this potentially lucrative area.

## Computer-Made Products

You can think of your computer as your own personal factory. It will produce products that you can sell to people. You have probably already seen or bought products made by a computer. Maybe you just haven't thought about using your own computer for this purpose. You should at least consider the possibilities. This area can provide lots of spare-time money-making opportunities if you're clever enough to take advantage of them.

If you've ever put a quarter in a machine to get a card with your biorhythm chart printed on it, you have bought a computer-made product. With a recent bill for a gasoline credit card, I received a full-color advertisement for a personalized biorhythm service. A computer-printed chart and analysis for the next twelve months could be provided for only $9.95 plus the ever-popular $1 for shipping and handling. Computerized horoscopes could be provided just as easily. Many stock market advisory services are based on the analysis and prediction by computer of stock prices. You may have even paid several dollars to have your picture printed out by a computer. You may have also seen patterns or artwork produced by computers. There is even a special purpose computer that can produce sculpture.

There may be a mail-order market for computer-printed pictures made from photographs. These pictures can be used on personalized T-shirts, mugs, greeting cards, or stationery. Special purpose computers to produce these pictures are currently quite expensive, but they will probably drop in price. You may eventually be able to buy attachments for your computer to provide such pictures. These pictures don't have to be limited to people. They can include houses, horses, or household pets.

Some years ago I had a friend who occasionally sold mathematically generated patterns to carpet and tile companies. Computer programs can be designed to generate an infinite number of patterns that would be suitable for carpets, tiles, wallpaper, or knitting. Unique computer-generated art could become more popular as the number of people involved with home computers grows. Computer-generated art can be produced with a dot matrix printer or a digital plotter, or they can be photographed from a TV display. A new opportunity to make money would involve producing personalized computer art. This might involve using a person's name or initials as the input to an art-producing program. The resulting art might comprise repetitive patterns evolving from the initials. It could also be a picture typed using only the letters in a name. The possibilities are endless.

Various types of word puzzles are always popular. You might be able to program your computer to design popular types of word puzzles that could be sold to a number of different magazines. Special interest magazines might be interested in word puzzles designed around sets of words relating to readers' specific interests.

Stock options lend themselves to computer analysis in a variety of ways. The analysis of stock price cycles by computer might be a useful trading tool. Any successful stock or option trading system that you develop for personal use provides a potential computer service that can be sold by mail. The requirements for becoming an investment adviser aren't very demanding. Maybe that's why there are so many poor ones around.

A new opportunity involves computer music and sound synthesis. Appropriate hardware is becoming readily available, and costs are dropping as well. Several small companies are making money by creating and selling unusual electronic sounds that are sold for use in radio station breaks and in commercials. You've probably heard them without realizing that creating them can be a profitable business.

Another unusual money-making opportunity involves computer-generated music. Some people believe that in the eighteenth century Mozart developed a system for automatically composing an almost unlimited number of different waltzes by throwing a pair of dice. Creation of pleasing music with random numbers was discussed in the Mathematical Games section of the April 1978 issue of *Scientific American*. You might consider programming your computer to create original music. Don't worry; you don't have to come up with a hit tune to make money. Instead, you can offer people cassette tapes containing custom written computer music derived from the letters in their names. Your computer can also be used to translate certain types of data into musical sequences of tones. You might try offering a cassette containing musical variations on the Dow Jones average. This would make a great conversation piece. You could advertise it in financial publications. People might like to hear what the crash of 1929 sounds like. They could also listen to the price of their favorite stock over the past month or year. It might make a catchy tune or help them predict where the stock is heading. If you give it some thought, you'll probably come up with lots more ideas for products your computer can produce.

## Sell Data, Not Programs

Creating and selling computer programs is an obvious money-making opportunity. Creating and selling data for computers may not be as obvious, but it represents another way to make money. There are two possible approaches. The first approach involves supplying data bases that can be used by various types of analysis programs. A good example is analysis of stock prices. Suppose you are developing and testing various stock or option trading systems. One of your needs is a file of price history for various stocks on which to test your system. Instead of tediously digging out this information and typing it in piece by piece, wouldn't you be willing to pay a nominal fee for suitable cassettes or discs?

Various tables of statistical data involving stocks, options, commodities, interest rates, or race results should appeal to people who develop analysis programs. This live test data should be provided in cassette or disc form for several of the most popular home computers. You might also offer a custom service for providing requested data or standard data in different formats. You could let your computer re-format the data for you.

The second approach to selling data involves looking at home computers in a slightly different way. You can view a home computer as you would a record player. The computer can play a cassette on the TV screen. This aspect of home computers opens up some more income opportunities for you. For example, you could prepare children's books in the form of cassettes. Playing the cassette would show the story on the TV screen along with pictures to illustrate it. Some animation could be included. The computer could initially ask for the names of the child, family, pets, and friends. These names could then be included in the story. Stories could even be varied each time they were played. A child could be asked to make plot decisions at various points in the story.

This type of material could be supplied in cassette or disc form. It should appeal to computer owners with children. This approach has another advantage. If you create a specific type of conventional program, you can sell it to a user only once. On the other hand, you can sell a variety of story cassettes or discs to the same family. Software publishers should become increasingly interested in this type of material. It will pay you to start thinking along these lines now. Remember that you don't have to be a very good programmer with this approach. The data presentation is what your customer is paying for. The currently popular adventure games are a perfect example of selling data rather than programs.

Obviously, the data that you play back using a home computer aren't limited to children's stories. Several home computer newsletters already are offered in cassette form. Interactive educational courses in a variety of areas can be offered in this form for children or adults. Other special interest newsletters are possible. One advantage over audio cassettes is the ability to freeze data on the TV screen. Look in stores to see what types of informational audio cassettes are being sold. You'll get ideas for similar data cassettes or discs for home computers. Money-making and self-improvement cassettes should be popular types.

As home computers become more widespread, you might have a market for greeting cassettes that owners of the same type of computer can send each other. You would supply appropriate fancy graphics and instructions for signing the sender's name.

It won't be long until many home computers include capabilities for the generation of music and voices. This will let you include music and voice in your story, information, or greeting cassettes and discs. You will also have a new opportunity to make money. This will involve writing, arranging, and coding music for home computers to play. Many owners will prefer to buy suitable music in cassette or disc form rather than translate it into a playable form themselves. You will probably have to pay royalties on previously published music you sell in this new form.

### Unique Attachments

Always remember that although computers can theoretically be programmed to do almost anything, in practice they're severely limited by existing input-output capabilities. Most owners of home computers will be interested in inexpensive attachments they can add to their computers to let them do new things. Most popular home computers have a plug for external attachments. In some cases, you can attach new devices to a home computer using the cassette recorder connections. You should probably be a hardware hacker if you want to design computer attachments. You'll also have to provide software that lets a customer use your attachments.

Many individuals and small companies design and sell novel attachments for popular home computers. If you create an interesting new attachment, you might be able to find a small company already in this business to make and sell it on a royalty basis. Computer attachments can also be sold in kit form to keep prices as low as possible. Kits may limit your market to hardware hackers.

Popular attachments for home computers can include calculator chips, clock chips, light pens, analog-to-digital input converters, digital-to-analog output converters, wireless remote control output devices, speech recognition input circuits, and ultrasonic or optical scanners. Other popular attachments involve output circuits for sound effects, music, or voice synthesis. Inexpensive circuits for connecting available low-cost printers to computers are possible. There is room for improved or lower cost designs in all these areas.

Inexpensive attachments for experimental or hobby uses should become increasingly popular. You might consider providing complete packages of the parts and attachments required for greenhouse control or model railroad control. Biofeedback experimentation packages might appeal to a number of people. Inexpensive light pistols for TV target shooting games don't seem to be currently available. How about a two-part attachment for target shooting games? An output attachment permits the computer to project moving light targets on a wall. The input attachment is comprised of a light gun for shooting at these projected targets. Special LED output displays or computer-controlled game boards might sell.

The whole area of inexpensive electromechanical devices has been pretty much neglected so far. One company is selling a small motorized turtle that can be attached to a computer by means of a cable. Prices start at several hundred dollars for a kit of parts. Why shouldn't a small, battery-operated, wireless, remote-controlled version be possible at much lower prices? Can you adapt various low-cost, remote-controlled toy robots or cars for use with microcomputers? You should be able to design a cheap mechanical arm that can be controlled by a microcomputer. It could be powered by inexpensive battery-operated motors. It could be used to move playing pieces on a game board, draw pictures, or experiment with positioning languages or programs. Cheap electromechanical lunar landing games or mouse mazes are possible. What else can you think of in this area?

Don't forget about some of the ideas discussed for construction articles in Chapter 5. Of particular interest is the design of special purpose microcomputers to attach to general purpose home computers. In the area of attachments for music or speech, the synthesis circuits could be reduced in cost and made easier to attach or use by integrating them into a special purpose microcomputer with built-in sequencing and control programs. Many chips for video games are actually special purpose computers that might be attached to general purpose home computers.

Keep your eyes open for new integrated circuit chips that could provide the basis for new attachments for home computers. Stay aware of new battery-operated toys and electronic games that could give you ideas for new attachments.

## Marketing Techniques

The home computer industry offers new opportunities for imaginative marketing approaches. Home computers are so new that manufacturers are using only the most obvious marketing approaches. They tend to sell computers through ads in computer magazines or leave the selling up to computer stores. There are, however, a variety of other ways to sell home computers. One of these, the party plan approach, was outlined at the end of Chapter 7. Another method would involve offering home computer hobbyists a sales commission. Who is more enthusiastic about home computers than existing owners? They like to show them to friends and demonstrate their uses. Why shouldn't computer companies use these existing salespeople and give them a chance to earn some extra money? If computer companies grow smarter and adopt either of these marketing approaches, it will provide you with an additional spare-time income opportunity.

You might consider another way of selling computers that was mentioned briefly in previous chapters. If you developed special interest software, you could use it to sell computers. If you worked out a really good stock or option trading system that ran on a low-cost computer, you could sell the complete software and hardware package by mail using ads in financial publications. You could advertise software–hardware packages for astrology or gambling in appropriate special interest magazines. A party game package could be advertised in *Playboy* or a children's educational package in *Parents' Magazine*.

If you don't want to get involved in selling hardware, you can still exploit this marketing approach. You develop the software and advertising part of the package and sell it to a computer company. Thinking in terms of large special interest markets will help you to develop software aimed specifically at selling hardware. This, in turn, will guarantee that computer companies will be interested in your software. Be sure to do your homework. Find out how many potential customers exist in a special interest area. Determine educational and income levels of the customers if possible. Discover their needs, design software to satisfy these needs, then tell the computer company about this great new market and show them specific advertising approaches.

Other selling opportunities involve reversing the preceding approach. Instead of selling computers in noncomputer magazines, sell existing products in computer magazines. Many people run part-time mail-order businesses from their homes. They sell a variety of products by advertising in magazines. Their degree of success is related to having the right product at the right price and writing a good advertisement that makes people want to send in their money.

You can start a mail-order business in which you already have an advantage over many other small mail-order operators. First, many of them aren't even aware that microcomputer magazines exist. Second, it takes someone who knows something about computers to talk effectively to people who are interested in them. Who knows more about the needs and desires of readers of magazines on home computers than you? If you give it some thought, you'll come up with a long list of items that would appeal to readers of computer magazines. You can expand your list by browsing through gift, novelty, and toy stores. When you see suitable products, add them to your list of products to sell.

Many readers of computer magazines are interested in computers but can't afford one. They *can* afford computer books and T-shirts. They might also buy funny computer novelties, posters, and sayings. I have seen a number of suitable items from time to time in stores. Look through the lines of greeting card and novelty companies to see what's available. A few computer-related games and toys exist but don't seem to be advertised in the microcomputer magazines at the present time.

You could sell books that aren't computer books in computer magazines. Books on puzzles, games, gambling, investing, inventing, busiⁿ ness, music theory, making money, and writing might sell. People interested in computers usually are fairly intelligent and have a wide variety of other interests. Many of them want to learn about new areas so they can develop new applications for their computers. Others are interested in making money with their computer. Hardware hackers might be interested in becoming inventors, and many programmers like games and puzzles of all types.

Many people are attracted to home computers because they like new electronic gadgets or toys. These same people represent a market for other, less expensive electronic gadgets and toys that would include novel calculators and the wide range of new electronic games and toys available now. You might even sell gold letters and racing stripes for computer owners who want to customize their hardware.

### Future Stuff

It's hard to talk about the future. No one is sure exactly how fast and in what direction the microcomputer industry will move. No one can be sure what new ideas will emerge from the large number of inventive and creative people who work with microcomputers. It's impossible to predict which new ideas will catch on and which ones will be greeted with resounding apathy. This section is a short random walk into the future.

Local computer centers were once thought to be the wave of the future. People could come in and rent time on computers to play games, learn, or do homework. Then computer stores came along, and there was a feeling that they would perform this service instead. Lower and lower prices for home computers now create some doubts about the need for such centers at all. A few owners of arcades containing coin-operated amusement devices are experimenting with the idea. One possibility for such centers would involve applications that aren't feasible with inexpensive home computers. Life-size starship simulators using large-screen displays, realistic controls, and computers might be extremely appealing. Multiple interactive simulators of space fighters would permit groups of players each to pilot his or her own ship and engage other players in battle. This could become the adult equivalent of amusement park bumper cars. Other interactive, highly realistic, multiple-player fantasy games could be conceived and implemented. These computer centers might become the electronic amusement parks of the future. They might emphasize mental stimulation more than physical thrills.

Inexpensive, direct communication with microcomputers can provide new business opportunities that would involve service centers where computer owners could call to have their computers immediately loaded with new programs or data from a library maintained by the center. Interactive computer games with friends over the telephone should become possible. You should also be able to hook in to multiple-player game nets by means of the local computer service center. The center would also permit people to leave messages for other subscribers in its data bank. This central data bank could also be used to advertise local computer-related products or services. Used equipment could be advertised this way. Closing stock prices and career planning data might be provided.

You should eventually see small handheld, battery-operated computers with about the same capabilities as today's low-cost BASIC systems. A small, liquid crystal display panel will replace the TV set. Small plug-in electronic storage modules will replace the cassette recorder. The cost of such computers may be $100 or less. The lower cost of the computer and larger numbers of owners will create a much larger demand for new software. Those programming and creative skills you're developing now won't go to waste in the future.

# 9

# Invent Your Way to Success

## General Considerations

After successfully trying inventing, writing, programming, computer development, and stock market speculation, my favorite spare-time money-making activity continues to be inventing. Because inventors comprise a persecuted minority group, this may only prove that I am a masochist. Many employed inventors have to sign away most of their rights before they're hired and don't even share in profits from their inventions. Independent inventors are preyed upon by unscrupulous invention brokers and ridiculed by the public. They are ignored or avoided by many companies. If they manage to scrape up the money for government and legal fees and actually get a patent, they still face problems in selling and protecting it. The government is happy to take the inventor's money to grant a patent. It has no interest at all in helping to protect the rights granted by the patent. If someone with money steals the invention, the inventor can go broke trying to defend his or her rights.

Our government always manages to voice deep concern over unemployment, decreasing productivity, and increasing trade deficits. It is willing to spend huge sums of money to study these problems. There seems to be no interest in passing laws to make life easier or provide incentives for individual inventors. Maybe politicians don't realize that individual inventors can create new products, jobs, and more efficient production methods if they are properly motivated. Maybe our elected representatives don't really care as much about the future of this country as they lead voters to believe. I prefer the view that they are merely confused. They probably believe that new ideas and inventions are created by abstract entities called companies. This confusion is hard to understand because even the patent office knows that inventions are conceived by individuals. Once this confusion is cleared up, our elected officials will undoubtedly waste little time in changing the system to motivate rather than discourage inventors.

On the positive side, inventing can be exciting and mentally stimulating, and it can have the appeal of buying a lottery ticket. You know the odds are stacked against you, but the possibility of that big payoff gives you something to look forward to. If you are successful, there is no high like the one you get from seeing your own creation on store shelves or in advertisements. The money you can make from a successful simple invention will even make you forget the years of frustration, rejection, and disappointment that preceded success. At the present time, royalty income from patents can be treated as long-term capital gains for income tax purposes. This results in considerable tax savings.

A patent gives you the exclusive right to make and sell your invention for seventeen years. You can sell or license these rights. Ideas can't be patented. You can patent new and novel electronic or mechanical devices or systems. The whole area of program patents is a mess. In general, you can't patent programs. It is, however, possible to patent certain types of special purpose computers. General purpose computers that are programmed to perform the same function may then be considered to be infringing the patent of the special purpose computer. If this sounds confusing, it is. Maybe someday this confusion will be straightened out.

If you think you have an idea for a patentable device, consult a local patent attorney. Avoid patent brokers. They advertise in magazines and newspapers. Have your attorney perform a patent search. This involves looking through previous patents to see if your device has already been invented. A good search may cost several hundred dollars. It's worth it. It won't guarantee that your invention is new, but it will bias the odds in your favor. Your attorney should then be able to give you an idea of your chances of obtaining a patent. Obtaining a simple patent can involve several thousand dollars, which includes your attorney's fees for preparing the patent application and various government fees. The patent office often rejects a patent application initially. The attorney then has to provide arguments in favor of granting your patent. This ritual of negotiation and compromise between the patent office and your attorney may take several years to complete. At the end of this time, you may or may not be granted a patent. Your attorney has no way of knowing how much argument, if any, will be required. This makes it impossible to determine the exact cost of obtaining a patent at the outset.

Selling a patent is often more difficult than obtaining one. More will be said about this later. If you plan to make and sell your invention yourself, you don't have to worry about licensing it. You'll have plenty of other things to worry about. If you want to sell or license your patent to a company, then you should try to sell it yourself or through a reputable agent. An agent shouldn't charge anything for trying to sell your patent.

If the patent is sold, the agent will get up to 50 per cent of the proceeds. Avoid agents or patent brokers who want money up front. There are many rip-off artists in this field. Gullible inventors keep them in business.

If you're interested in becoming a freelance inventor, the following books will provide varying degrees of help.

*Yates' Guide to Successful Inventing* (1967) by Raymond F. Yates, published by Funk & Wagnalls.

*Inventor's Complete Guide Book* (1959) by Arthur Liebers, published by Key Publishing Co.

*Inventor's Handbook* (1969) by T. W. Fenner & J. L. Everett, published by Chemical Publishing Co., Inc.

*The Successful Inventor's Guide* (1965) by K. O. Kessler & N. Carlisle, published by Prentice-Hall, Inc.

*Complete Guide to Making Money With Your Ideas* (1976) by R. E. Paige, published by Barnes & Noble Books.

*How To Become a Successful Inventor* (1973) by E. P. McNair & J. E. Schwenck, published by Hastings House Publishers, Inc. This is one of my favorites.

Some of these books may be out of print by now. Check with your local bookstore. You should be able to find other books on inventing in stores and libraries. There have been changes in patent laws and fees since most of these books were written. A good local patent attorney is your best source of up-to-date information on procedures and costs. Your attorney should also be consulted about sales or licensing agreements. There are many pitfalls for the beginner in this area. Consult your attorney to make sure that a specific contract is worded so that income can be treated as long-term capital gains.

One potential pitfall is your relation with your full-time employer. If you're an employed engineer or scientist, you may have signed a contract giving your employer rights to subsequent inventions. You must obtain a written release for specific personal inventions. Also make sure that your personal inventing doesn't make use of any of your employer's know-how, time, or physical facilities. If it does, your employer can have valid claims to rights in your invention.

## Simple Inventions Pay

Anyone can become an inventor. This doesn't mean that all areas of inventing are practical for everyone. Inventing a new microcomputer or automobile engine would involve technical capabilities that most people don't have. This section discusses an area for inventing that is open to everybody. It provides you with the best opportunities to make money whether you're a beginner or an expert. This inventing opportunity involves simple new games, gadgets, toys, and puzzles. Let's look at the reasons why this area provides your best chance for success.

Inventions can be classified into four types as follows:

1. Minor simple inventions.
2. Major simple inventions.
3. Minor complex inventions.
4. Major complex inventions.

Major inventions are fundamental kinds that provide the basis for new industries or have a major impact on the world. There have been relatively few major inventions. The wheel, radio, TV, the internal combustion engine, the telephone, and the electronic digital computer are examples of major inventions. The majority of inventions are minor. They involve improvements on major inventions, or they are small conveniences. Most games, gadgets, toys, and puzzles fall into this category.

When you see a simple invention, you usually say, "Why didn't I think of that?" The idea is obvious once someone has it. Implementation of the idea is relatively easy. Paper clips and the Ouija board are in this category. Complex inventions involve lots of parts and can take years to perfect. Copying machines, video tape recorders, and typewriters all belong in this category.

Your chances of coming up with a major new invention such as an antigravity or teleportation machine are pretty small. If you did invent one of these devices, you would probably antagonize the entire transportation industry. You might have to spend the rest of your life defending your rights in a major invention. This has happened in the past. The odds are stacked against you. Let's eliminate major inventions as a goal for spare-time income.

Complex inventions usually involve years of expensive development effort. Many inventors devote their entire lives and a lot of money to perfecting one complex invention. A high level of skill is usually required. Patents are expensive. Not too many companies may want to buy it after you perfect it. Rapidly changing technology can make it obsolete before you can profit from it. Large competing companies are skilled at finding ways around your patent. The odds are stacked against you. Let's eliminate complex inventions as a viable spare-time money making activity.

The only inventions left to consider are the minor simple ones. High levels of skill aren't usually required. Development time and expense can be low. It's usually not worth the effort and expense to try to steal them. All you need is a good idea; therefore, large research and development groups in major companies don't have any advantage over you in this area.

Now we have to decide what specific area provides the best chance for you to make money with minor simple inventions. To decide this, we'll examine the fundamental mistake most amateur inventors make. Amateur inventors have come up with amazing variety of extremely clever and novel ideas over the years. If you don't believe this, just look through old patents. Why did most of these inventors fail to achieve financial success? The reason is simple. They invented things that nobody wanted to buy. Successful inventors avoid this mistake either by accident or by using the proper approach. You are going to succeed by taking the proper approach.

The proper approach identifies those persons who will buy your invention first. Then you can proceed to invent something aimed at this buyer. If you want to license inventions to existing companies, you must find those that are anxious to buy inventions from independent inventors. Most large companies are happy with their research and development departments. They are concerned with improving existing products rather than in developing new products. These companies aren't receptive to outside inventors, and most of them won't even look at ideas submitted by outsiders. If your sister-in-law happens to be the president of one of these companies, you might stand a chance. Otherwise, forget about them as a possible customer for your patent. There is one group of companies who are not only receptive to outside inventors but who depend on them. These companies are those that produce games, gadgets, toys, and puzzles. They need a constant flow of unique ideas to stay in business. They have bought thousands of ideas from independent inventors in the past. The market for these types of inexpensive products is very large. You can make a $50,000 profit on a simple game or gadget that's not even a best seller.

Although most companies in this area buy inventions from outsiders, not all of them will deal with amateur inventors. After you've successfully sold some inventions, you will have become a professional and more doors will open for you. An agent can be helpful in gaining entry to some companies. This is similar to the situation in the publishing industry. Many book publishers will look only at submissions made by agents or previously published authors.

One of your best sources of information on the toy and game industry is a magazine called *Playthings*. It's published monthly by Geyer McAllister Publications, Inc., 51 Madison Ave., New York NY 10010. It can keep you up to date on what's happening in the toy and game industry. They also publish an annual directory issue which lists toy and game companies, part suppliers, and independent designers. *Toy & Hobby World* is a similar publication. Its address is 124 E. 40th Street, New York NY 10016.

Your computer knowledge can give you an advantage in inventing new games, gadgets, toys, or puzzles. Many inventors succeed by applying knowledge from one field of activity to another field. You can apply your knowledge of computers to invent new games, toys, or puzzles of general interest. You can also invent games or gadgets that would appeal specifically to people interested in computers. Your inventions have to satisfy needs or desires at appropriate prices in order to succeed.

Paper clips and other gadgets or tools usually satisfy obvious needs. Always be on the lookout for specific new needs and simple ways to satisfy them. Games, puzzles, and toys often satisfy less obvious human needs or desires. These needs involve popularity, prestige, learning, mental stimulation, vicarious thrills, relaxation, or emotional release. You can really let your imagination run wild in attempting to create inventions to satisfy desires of this type.

If you come up with a good idea, consult a patent attorney and have a patent search performed to verify that your idea is really new. You must then decide if it can be made for an appropriate price, how large the market is, and whether it would fit into the product lines of existing companies. If the price would be too high, forget it. If there isn't a large market, forget it. For example, a game that would appeal only to five-year-old boys would have a much smaller market than one aimed at children and adults of both sexes. If it doesn't fit into the product lines of existing companies, you may have to produce and sell it yourself to make any money.

If it looks like the invention could make enough money to justify the cost of a patent application, have your attorney proceed to prepare one. In the meantime, you can start trying to sell your invention to a company on a patent-pending basis. You must have complete documentation and a working model of professional appearance. Write letters to appropriate companies asking if they are interested in looking at a new product idea. Don't provide any pictures, drawings, or detailed information with this letter. You will be ignored by some companies. Others will send a letter saying they're not interested in new ideas at the present time. Some will send you a standard submission form for new products. You can then submit the details of your invention accompanied by this form. Submit your idea to only one company at a time. Don't send a model unless its asked for. Companies can take up to a year to evaluate your invention before finally accepting it or rejecting it. It pays to have a number of simple inventions making the rounds in parallel. Don't be discouraged by rejections. I have received as many as fifty rejections before finding a company to license an invention.

Game, gadget, toy, and puzzle inventing can be a lucrative spare-time money-making activity. It can also be a lot of fun. If you can sell one invention, the profits can be used to finance new ones. If you are imaginative, take the right approach, have patience, and aren't frustrated easily, you may be a potential inventor. You only have to think up another *Instant Insanity* puzzle or a *Mastermind* game to become rich.

The next two sections discuss other potentially lucrative areas for inventors in which microcomputers can be used. These areas require higher levels of technical ability and provide lower chances for success. They are worth considering only because of the possibly large payoffs involved.

## Communicating with Computers

New input-output inventions are a major need in the microcomputer industry. Appropriate inventions can stimulate industry growth. Lack of new inventions in the input output area will retard the growth of the microcomputer industry. Don't be too optimistic about your chances in this area. Most of the needs have been known for years, and a lot of clever people have failed to satisfy them.

A computer can process stored data very rapidly, which makes it ideal for handling large amounts of data. Very inexpensive data storage devices that can maximize the usefulness of inexpensive microcomputers are an acute need. Audio cassette recorders are the cheapest bulk storage devices currently in use. They cost about $50, and they are slow and unreliable. They are serial storage devices. You have to search the tape in serial fashion to find a desired piece of information, which makes them impractical for many applications. Floppy discs also store data magnetically and provide semirandom access. The computer can find a large chunk of data almost immediately, which makes floppy discs good for many applications that cassette recorders can't handle. Unfortunately, units that use floppy discs currently cost about $500. This is more than the cost of some microcomputers. If you can invent a device that costs less than $50, stores several million pieces of data, and lets a microcomputer find any piece of data in a second or so, you are on your way to becoming rich.

Another need also involves data storage. A general purpose computer needs different programs to be useful. These programs have to be recorded in or on something so that they can be stored on shelves, sold, or sent through the mail. These programs also have to be loaded into a computer to make them useful. The cheapest form of program storage involves printing the programs on sheets of paper in book or magazine form. They then have to be typed into a computer by hand. What's really needed is a cheap form of program storage that is machine readable. Some experiments with printed machine-readable codes have been tried. Plug-in Read Only Memory (ROM) modules have been used but this approach requires a large number of copies of the same program to get the cost down to reasonable levels.

What is needed is a storage method that is inexpensive, machine-readable, and external. A microcomputer owner should also have the ability to save custom or one-of-a-kind programs in the same form for later use or sale. Punched cards, punched paper tape, magnetic strips, magnetic discs, cassettes, and erasable ROM chips are currently used for this purpose. They all have disadvantages and are currently too expensive. A new cheap approach can open up vast new microcomputer markets.

Printed microcomputer output is needed for many applications. There is currently no cheap way to provide suitable output in printed form. There is no inexpensive way for computers to draw pictures on paper. TV sets are relatively expensive display devices for many applications. New and inexpensive output devices could fill real needs.

There are also a number of input device needs. There is no inexpensive reliable way to talk to computers yet. Wouldn't you like a $300 typewriter that you could dictate letters to? It would have cost me at least that much to have the manuscript for this book typed. Inexpensive devices to read typed or printed material would be useful. Devices to easily measure brain waves or blood pressure could expand microcomputer use.

By now you should realize that there are plenty of unfilled needs in the area of input-output and bulk storage. As you learn more about computers and start using your own computer, you'll discover lots of unfilled needs for yourself. Many concern less expensive ways of doing things. This is a fertile field for inventors.

## Special Purpose Computers

Another excellent area for inventors is that of special purpose computers. The market for new special purpose microcomputers is exploding. Companies can't keep up with the demand and are searching for new ideas. These special purpose microcomputers range from expensive instruments down to low-cost toys and games. Not all segments of the market are expanding as rapidly as others. This is a difficult area for beginners and independent inventors to compete in. Most of the new special purpose microcomputer products will be developed by large companies that have the required resources. To compete in this area you will need a high level of technical ability and the resources required to develop product prototypes. It's not impossible for independent inventors to succeed in this area, just difficult. The first home video game was developed by an independent inventor as was one of the first microcomputer board games.

You should probably concentrate on special purpose microcomputers related to toys, games, or home computers. You may be able to simulate your invention on a general purpose computer to develop, evaluate, test, or demonstrate it. You should become familiar with inexpensive chips that can be used to implement your idea. The major part of your invention will usually be the input-output approach and algorithms. You can construct a physical model of the invention and program a general purpose computer to simulate the electronic portion. This will allow you to demonstrate the invention to potential buyers. If a large company likes the idea, it can have custom chips made to implement the electronics. A system patent might be obtained for your invention. This type of patent involves novel combinations of existing devices to perform a new and useful function. A microcomputer can be considered as a single device in a system. You may also be able to think of useful, new, special purpose microcomputers for educational purposes.

Toy and game companies aren't the only customers for new special purpose microcomputer ideas. Companies making integrated circuits could be interested in new ideas that look as though they would sell millions of a new type of chip.

Another general approach to coming up with special purpose microcomputer ideas involves building a microcomputer into existing devices or products. Look at existing toys, games, or household appliances. Ask yourself how adding an inexpensive microcomputer chip could improve them. Audio equipment companies are starting to offer computerized turntables and cassette recorders. The microcomputer allows them to be programmed to play preselected sequences of songs and skip selected sections of records or tapes. Automobile companies are building microcomputer chips into cars for engine control or fancy dashboard displays. Microcomputers are being designed into washing machines, dryers, stoves, blenders, electronic organs, telephones, sewing machines, and typewriters. Can you think of other appliances that might be combined with microcomputer chips? Look through toy stores. Maybe you'll see some existing toys or games that could become new products if a microcomputer were added to them.

The area of special purpose microcomputers doesn't offer the average reader many inventing opportunities so it is not discussed in any further detail. It is included only as a possible area of interest for readers who happen to be highly skilled computer professionals. Even many of these readers won't be able to take advantage of opportunities in this area because of potential conflicts of interest with their full-time employers.

# 10

## Making Your Money Grow

### Letting Money Work for You

Money is a fundamental problem in most people's lives. Many people don't even realize this fact. Most people think only of the material possessions that money can buy. The real importance of money is the freedom and security it provides. It can give you the freedom to work at whatever activity you enjoy. It gives you the freedom to do what you want when you want. It even gives you the freedom to live in a cave with no material possessions if that's what turns you on. Money can buy happiness!

As a computer designer, I receive letters from computer hobbyists who invariably have the same type of question. How can they cheaply modify an inexpensive microcomputer so that it performs as well as more expensive computers? People who spend a disproportionate amount of time searching for ways to save money on household purchases have the same problem. The basic problem or question is, "How can I afford something I can't afford?" The answer is simple: Increase your income to the point at which you can afford what you want. This book was written to help you do this. If you want to increase your income, then you should start thinking about making new dollars instead of saving existing pennies. This is probably contrary to what you've been taught all your life. You will just have to change your thinking. Money making can be a fascinating new hobby. There's nothing shameful about making money. You can do more good in this world with money than you can without it.

You have five resources you can use to make money. They are knowledge, skill, time, imagination, and money. You can sell or rent your knowledge, skill, or time. You can use your imagination to create profitable ideas. You should also make sure that your money is always working for you as well. As you make extra money in your spare time, it becomes increasingly important to put it to work for you. Letting money sit in savings accounts is not an effective way to put it to work. Suppose a savings account pays 6 per cent interest, the inflation rate is 8 per cent, and you are in a 25 per cent tax bracket. Any money you have in the savings account will not be increasing at 6 per cent per year. It will be shrinking at an approximate rate of 3.5 per cent per year. This is not a good way to make your money grow. It is not even a good way just to hold on to it.

One way of putting your money to work involves substituting money for your time. If you can average $10 an hour writing programs in your spare time, then paying somebody $5 an hour to cut your grass for you is putting your money to work for a possible 100 per cent return.

Another good way to put your money to work is investing it in your money-making activities. Buying books like this one is a good example. If this book stimulates you to write one simple article that you sell for only $50, you have made your money grow by about 1000 per cent. Money spent on magazines and other books that can improve your money-making abilities is an excellent way to put small amounts of money to work for you.

As your ability to make money improves, you will have an increasing amount of extra money to put to work. The rest of this chapter deals with other ways to put money to work for you. As you make more money, always put a small amount aside for high-risk, high-return situations. Large amounts of money should be put to work only in situations of lower risk and smaller potential return.

### Become a Silent Partner

If you're married, your spouse has probably often given you this advice. You can put money to work by buying a piece of somebody else's money-making activity. Your success in this area will depend on how good your judgment is. You will have to judge both the people and the activity they are involved in. You will also have to be watching for opportunities. Your best chance to find these opportunities will probably involve personal contacts made through clubs or consulting.

Many times an independent inventor will have trouble raising money to finance a patent application. You can supply the required money for a share in future income from the patent. Evaluate the invention using Chapter 9 as a guide. Also evaluate the inventor's ability to be realistic and follow through on selling the invention.

As the microcomputer industry grows, there will be thousands of new small businesses formed. Small computer-related companies and stores represent investment opportunities for you. Some stores will be national franchise operations. You might consider absentee ownership of such a store. Investing in a newsletter operation or a new local microcomputer repair shop are other possibilities.

You might have an idea for a small business that you don't want to run yourself. You could find one or more partners. You would contribute the basic idea along with money, knowledge, and advice. Your partners would actually run the business. Make sure that everyone involved has to put up some money. This means everyone has something to lose if the business fails. Also make sure that everyone is motivated by being able to share in any profits. People have made a lot of money by forming new companies in rapidly growing industries and selling out after the company has become established. New small businesses are a high risk area. Don't invest more than you can afford to lose.

### Computer Industry Stocks

Sometimes you can make a lot of money by speculating on the stocks of companies involved in the microcomputer industry. These stocks can involve large or small companies. You look for companies that have come up with a new microcomputer product or service that looks as though it will be popular. You then buy stock in the company, keep your fingers crossed that it will go up, and sell it if it does. You had also better sell it if it doesn't.

There are two pitfalls to watch out for. It is difficult for a single new product to have a significant effect on the profits of a large diversified company. You have to evaluate carefully the likely effect of a new microcomputer product on the price of a large company's stock. The second pitfall involves the cyclic behavior of the stock market as a whole. For the past several decades the majority of stock prices have moved up and down in a four- to five-year cycle. Major price lows have occurred every four to five years. This behavior appears to be related to the four-year political cycle and attempts by the government to manipulate the economy. As a result of the cyclic behavior of stock prices, you have to watch the timing of any stock purchases carefully. If a company comes up with a new microcomputer product during the down portion of the general stock market cycle, you will have less chance to make money with the stock. If the new product appears during the up phase of the market cycle, you stand a good chance to profit. Looking at any long-term chart of stock averages will immediately identify these price cycles for you.

Radio Shack is a division of Tandy Corporation. It is a good example of how you can make money on microcomputer stocks. Tandy stock is traded on the New York Stock Exchange. In the last half of 1977, when Tandy announced the TRS-80 home computer, their stock was trading around $30 a share. If you had bought fifty shares for $1,500, you could have sold them for $3,000 one year later for a 100 per cent profit. If you had waited until as late as March of 1978, you could have bought six-month $35 call options for $2.50. If you had bought 500 of these options for $1,250, you could have sold them four months later for about $7,000. It would have probably paid to wait anyway to verify that the TRS-80 would be popular. We discuss options in more detail later. Opportunities like this don't come along too often. It will pay you to be watching for them when they do.

You can expect to see more new microcomputers in the future. Don't forget about companies making chips and input-output devices. They will also benefit from the growing popularity of microcomputers. Look for new companies in the microcomputer industry. Stocks of new companies can sometimes make money for you.

## Computer Portfolio Management

The preceding section discussed investing in stocks related to microcomputers. This section discusses using your home computer to help you make money in the stock market. In the old days you could buy the stock of a good company and hold it for ten or twenty years to make money. These days even the price of IBM stock goes up and down by large amounts every few years so that you have to trade stocks over shorter periods of time to maximize your profits. Your computer can be an invaluable aid for making money in the stock market. Before you can put your money and your computer to work in this area, you should plan to spend at least a year learning about the stock market. The following books can get you started learning about this fascinating area.

The Art of Low Risk Investing (1977) by Michael G. Zahorchak is a good book that shows how moving averages can help you in buying and selling stocks. The moving average approach lends itself to implementation by the home computer. This book is published by Van Nostrand Reinhold Company.

The New Money Dynamics (1978) by Venita Van Caspel covers a wide range of investing topics. It's published by Reston Publishing Company, Inc., a Prentice-Hall Company. This book isn't limited to the stock market. It's a good introduction to personal money management in general.

Modern Strategy for Successful Investing (1974) by K. V. Smith and D. K. Eiteman discusses investment portfolio construction and management. It's published by Dow Jones–Irwin, Inc. Homewood IL 60430. This is an excellent reference book. It emphasizes fundamental approaches to company analysis.

*How Charts Can Help You in the Stock Market* (1962) by William L. Jiler explains technical analysis using stock price chart patterns. It's published by Trendline, a division of Standard & Poor's Corp.

*The Thinking Investor's Guide to the Stock Market* (1978) by Kiril Sokoloff is a general discussion of stock market investing. It's published by McGraw-Hill Book Company.

*Guide to Intelligent Investing* (1977) by J. B. Cohen, E. D. Zinbarg, and A. Zeikel is another good book on stock market investing. It's published by Dow Jones–Irwin. It discusses risk management along with other subjects concerning stocks.

*Buy Low, Sell High* (1978) by John E. Mahoney is another interesting stock market book. It's published by Pagurian Press Limited, Suite 1106, 335 Bay Street, Toronto, Canada. It discusses a specific system for buying and selling stocks that could easily be adapted for use on a home computer.

There are many other books about the stock market that can help you. Look through bookstores and libraries to find them. Your local stock broker can also help you to learn about the stock market and advise you on various sources of stock price charts and company evaluations.

Playing the stock market can be a fascinating game. You should not refer to it in these terms when talking to financial people. There is some question as to whether short-term stock price variations are predictable or random. *The Profit Magic of Stock Transaction Timing* (1970) by J. M. Hurst points out that stock price behavior may involve the cumulative effect of a number of cyclic components. Whether this view can consistently let you make money remains to be seen. This book was based on hundreds of hours of analysis of computer stock prices. It's published by Prentice-Hall, Inc.

Your best chance of making money with stocks probably involves watching the four- to five-year cycle of stock prices. Look for stocks in financially sound companies that seem to follow this cycle. After a major low in the cycle seems to have been reached, buy good stocks. Everyone else will be selling. After a year or two, sell all your stocks and wait for the next low to occur. Your computer can help you compare company and stock price statistics. It can help you evaluate investment alternatives during bear markets. You can set up a matrix of risk–reward parameters for a variety of stocks and other investments. You can then use the computer to analyze the expected return for various investment mixes.

The next section discusses another way to make profits in the stock market. You can use this approach whether stocks are going up or down. It has a higher profit potential, but it also involves much higher risks.

## The Hottest Game in Town

Listed stock options are only a few years old. Analyzing the large variety of option strategies and trading systems is an excellent application of the home computer. A call option is essentially a bet that a stock will go up. You might pay $2 for a $60 call option on a share of General Motors' stock when the stock is worth $55 a share. The option will expire in some period of time. Listed options are sold with lives of three, six, and nine months. Just before your GM option expires, it will be worthless if the stock is trading at or below $60 a share. If the stock is worth more than $60 a share, the option value will be the difference between the stock price and $60. The $2 was what it cost you to bet that the stock would move up over $60 during the life of the option. If, after you paid your $2, the stock moved up to $70 before your option expired, you could sell the option for at least $10. If the stock didn't move above $60 during the life of the option, you could lose your $2 unless you sold the option at a lower price before expiration. Put options are similar, but you are betting that the stock price will go down during the life of the option.

If you are interested in stock options, the following books will teach you about them.

*The Stock Options Manual* (1975) by Gary L. Gastineau is one of the best option reference books. It's published by McGraw-Hill Book Company. It discusses option pricing and strategies for using options. It was written by an experienced professional.

*The Dow Jones–Irwin Guide to Put and Call Options* (1975) by Henry K. Clasing, Jr. is another good reference book on options.

*How to Make Money Trading Listed Puts* (1978) by Lin Tso provides lots of examples of various option stategies. It's published by Frederick Fell Publishers, Inc., New York.

*Buying Options* (1976) by Anthony Rodolakis and Nicholas Tetrick discusses option trading. It's published by Reston Publishing Company, Inc., a Prentice-Hall Company. The trading approach presented uses probability theory. This type of approach is a good application of a home computer.

A variety of stategies for using listed options is possible. You can buy or sell puts or calls. You can use various combinations of buying and selling options together with buying stocks. It almost requires a computer to compare the risk–reward potentials of all possible combinations. This area provides an excellent way to use your computer.

Option prices are directly related to stock prices. Option trading should be based on short-term swings of stock prices. Relatively small variations in stock prices can result in large option profits or losses because of the leverage that options provide. You can modify any stock trading system for use with options.

There is a variety of automatic systems for buying and selling stocks. They can use moving averages or other technical analysis approaches to provide buy and sell signals. You should first look at such systems and decide which one looks best for you. This decision will involve how easy the system is to use and how much time you'll have to devote to it. Hourly or daily trading systems aren't any good if you want to devote only an hour or so each week to your stock or option trading activity.

After finding a set of trading rules or a system that looks good for you, get ready to take the next step. This involves programming your computer to test the system. Pick several stocks that are good candidates for use with the system. These are generally stocks of large, financially sound companies. They should exhibit large price swings and have listed options associated with them. Program your computer to apply your trading rules to these stocks over at least the last six years of price history. You can try variations of your trading rules to maximize average annual profit. If you find a system that works, you can start using it with actual money. Never commit more than 10 per cent of your trading funds to any one trade. This will let you survive a string of losses. Make sure you use the computer to give you buy and sell signals. Always obey the computer's instructions without letting your judgment interfere. The major advantage of using your computer involves eliminating emotion from your decisions.

In a brief discussion of this type it's impossible to go into all the details required for success. The books listed in this chapter can help you learn what you need to know. I believe that computer-aided option trading can be a good spare-time money-making activity. You can trade the options of a few volatile stocks during both bull and bear markets. Your optimum trading period will be four to ten weeks. There is usually enough stock price variation within this period to make option profits.

Your computer can be a big help in calculating the probability of making a profit on individual trades. If you trade only when the odds are in your favor, you should come out ahead in the long run. Your computer can also eliminate emotion from your trading decisions. Option trading is a high-risk activity. Never dedicate more than 10 per cent of your available money to this activity.

## The Ultimate Money Machine

Most traders lose money for a variety of reasons. A major reason involves emotional reactions by the trader. Failure to take a series of small losses because you feel a turnaround is about to occur is one way to lose money. Getting emotionally caught up in buying or selling panics is another good way to lose money. It causes you to buy close to tops and sell near bottoms. Putting your trading rules or system on a computer helps eliminate emotional trading decisions and increases your chance for success.

Even if you run your trading system on a computer, you have to carry out the computer's instructions. I have often ignored my computer and suffered losses as a result. Current technology makes it possible entirely to eliminate your emotions from the system. Telephone stock and option price quotation systems exist for feeding current prices directly into your home computer. It is also possible for a computer to phone buy and sell orders directly to a broker. Inexpensive hardware for this purpose should be available in the near future. With a system like this you just let your computer trade options for you. You're free to do anything you want while your computer sits at home in its corner building up the money in your trading account for you. This is the ultimate money machine. Unlike a personal printing press for twenty dollar bills, this money machine is completely legal. It represents the perfect application of home computers.

How realistic is such a money machine? The hardware already exists. You can compare various stock, commodity, or option trading systems against real historical data to test their performance yourself. Some money management companies have claimed to be using computerized trading systems with considerable success. If your trading period averages out to eight weeks, you have to average only a 5 per cent profit per trade to achieve a 30 per cent gain for the year. You can use a trading system based on actual probabilities of measured stock price swings. Trading only when the odds are in your favor should be the same as playing a roulette wheel biased slightly in your favor. Over the long run you almost *have* to come out ahead.

Whether such a system is possible, is something you will have to decide for yourself. It would appear to be an interesting target for the application of home computers. You will learn a lot in the process. Maybe some people already have a system like this working for them but aren't talking about it. Would you?

Much of this chapter has discussed stock and option markets. None of the advice provided guarantees that you will make money.

# 11

## Working at Home

### Self-Discipline

If you have spent your life going to school and working for other people, you will have to make some personal adjustments. To pursue spare-time money-making activities, you will have to learn to structure your own time, provide your own motivation, and risk your own money. These are hard adjustments for most people to make.

You will succeed only if you are highly motivated. Some of the popular self-improvement books can be helpful in this area. You've probably seen many of them in bookstores. Now read some of them. They teach positive thinking and tell stories of how other people became successful. They should provide you with inspiration. Many of your friends will belittle your efforts. Ignore them. Try to enlist your family as supportive partners.

You will have to make efficient use of your spare time to succeed. Steal time from chores, recreation, and other hobbies. Try not to steal time from your family. Make sure that a small percentage of spare-time profits is devoted to rewarding yourself or your family with small luxuries whenever possible. The bulk of your profits should always be used to expand your spare-time business activities.

Think of your spare-time money-making activities as a hobby. You can allocate a certain amount of money to spend on this area the same as you would for any hobby. You can also think of your spare-time activity as a business in which you will invest a certain amount of money. Watch your expenses carefully. Executives of large companies who control huge sums of other people's money often have trouble managing their own resources.

You must discipline yourself to devote a specific amount of time each day or each week to your part-time money-making activities. You should keep records. They will tell you what your expenses and profits are. Records of where you have submitted programs or articles are essential. Don't run your business in your head. Write everything down. Keep a separate bank account for your spare-time business money.

Make sure you keep your spare-time business separate from your full-time job. Your full-time job provides the financial base for spare-time money-making activities. Your full-time job should always receive top priority.

### Equipment and Supplies

You will need to purchase books and magazines for educational and planning purposes. This is your most important initial investment. Next you will need to arrange a home office of some sort. This need be no more than a desk and some bookshelves in an out-of-the-way spot where you can have a quiet place to think and work without distractions. It will also permit you to keep all the material associated with your part-time business activities in one place. A separate work area has another advantage. You will not be working continuously for long periods of time. If you're writing an article, it will probably be done by stealing an hour here and an hour there. If you have to clean up after every work session and get everything out again prior to the next short session, you'll never finish. Having a separate place to work solves this problem.

It's hard to imagine any part-time money-making activity that doesn't require a typewriter. Try to get an electric one with cartridge ribbons. You should also make sure that it has a wide carriage that will take 8½-by-11-inch paper the long way. Paper this size is handy for typing tables. A typewriter can also be useful for other family members, so it is a worthwhile investment. If you have lots of money, you might consider adding an IBM Selectric typewriter to your computer. This addition will give you a word-processing system that can make preparing letters, articles, and books a lot easier.

You should have letterheads printed for your use. They are inexpensive and add a professional touch to your correspondence. You may be able to find a local artist or art student to design a distinctive one for you. Business cards can also be handy in many cases and are inexpensive to obtain.

Eventually you will find a copying machine invaluable. You can buy thermal types for about $300. A used one will cost less. They can be used to make copies of letters, articles, contracts, and any other printed material. With rub-on letters and a copy machine you can prepare professional looking title pages and advertisements for your work.

If you're a hardware hacker, you will need parts, a soldering iron, and a scope in addition to normal office supplies and equipment.

## More Resources

Get to know your local fast printing shop. They can do offset printing, letterheads, and photo copies for you. They are inexpensive and fast. If you are involved with inventing, you will need a local patent attorney. Eventually you should find a local certified public accountant to help you with tax matters. Avoid the type of tax preparation services for the mass consumer that become popular during the first quarter of every year.

The following books provide interesting reading if you're going to be involved with spare-time money-making activities of any kind.

*The Home Office Guide* (1968) by Leon Henry, Jr. provides lots of tips and advice on working at home. It's distributed by Arco Publishing Company, Inc., New York.

*Working for Yourself* (1977) by Geof Hewitt gives a number of examples of people who have successfully gone into business for themselves. It's published by Rodale Press, Emmaus, PA.

*How to Make Big Money at Home in Your Spare Time* (1971) by Scott Witt lists a number of spare-time money-making ideas. It's published by Parker Publishing Company, Inc., West Nyack, NY.

*Think and Grow Rich* (1960) by Napoleon Hill is a classic inspirational book that can help motivate you. It's published by Fawcett Publications, Inc. *How to Make More Money* (1953) by Marvin Small is another classic of the same type. It's published by Pocket Books, Inc., New York.

As stated previously in this book, your imagination is your major resource. Books and magazines can stimulate this resource into working for you. Read everything you can lay your hands on that is related to making money or to microcomputers. You never know exactly when you'll come up with a simple idea that can make you rich.

## Rewards

This book is primarily concerned with freelance money-making opportunities in the rapidly growing microcomputer industry. In order to be successful, you will have to become a home computer hobbyist. This means that you will be continuously increasing your knowledge and skills in the microcomputer field. As you begin trying to turn your hobby into a spare-time money-making enterprise, you will also be meeting new people, learning about companies, and discovering trends in the microcomputer industry. Your primary goals will be extra income and fun. Your new hobby will also provide you with a number of fringe benefits.

No matter what your full-time occupation is now, it will sooner or later be affected in some way by computer technology. This means that your increasing knowledge of computers stands an excellent chance of helping you in your job. Your hobby can improve your chances for a raise in pay or for a promotion. You should try to find potential micro-computer applications related to your job. If your company isn't aware of the possible uses of microcomputers, you might become the resident expert.

Your microcomputer knowledge, experience, and increasing awareness of opportunities could help you find a better job with more opportunity for personal growth. Personal contacts made during your spare-time activities may be useful if you're ever faced with the need to find a new job.

Developing your spare-time money-making abilities offers other rewards. You can beat high rates of inflation and taxes. You can obtain a feeling of real accomplishment. You will have increased security based on your ability to earn money on your own. Spare-time money-making activities can make retirement fun. Spare-time money-making can lead to self-confidence, new friends, and a richer life. If this book helps you achieve any of these rewards, it has served its purpose.

# Index